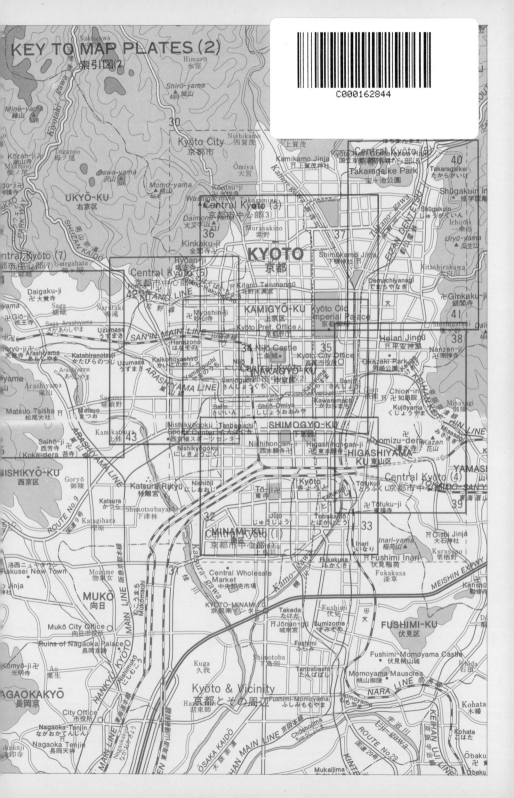

KEY TO MAP PLATES (2)
索引図(2)

Distributed in the United States by Kodansha America, Inc.,
114 Fifth Avenue, New York, N.Y. 10011,
and in the United Kingdom and continental Europe
by Kodansha Europe Ltd.,
95 Aldwych, London WC2B 4JF.
Published by Kodansha International Ltd., 17-14 Otowa 1-chome,
Bunkyo-ku, Tokyo 112, and Kodansha America, Inc.
Produced by Atushi Umeda., 3-6 Tama-cho 2-chome, Chofu-city, Tokyo

96 97 98 99 10 9 8 7 6 5 4 3 2

ISBN 4-7700-1610-7

「この地図の作成に当っては、建設省国土地
理院発行の2.5万分の1地形図、50万分の1
地方図を使用しました。(測量法第30条に基
づく成果使用承認　平4近使、第53号)」

KYŌTO-ŌSAKA

A BILINGUAL ATLAS
関西二ヵ国語アトラス

目　次

CONTENTS

inki Area　近畿地方 ·················· 2

eihanshin District
京阪神地区 ·················· 4

saka & Kobe　大阪・神戸 ·················· 6

outhern Ōsaka & Wakayama
大阪南部・和歌山 ·················· 8

yōto Basin　京都盆地 ·················· 10

ara Basin　奈良盆地 ·················· 12

kashi & Himeji　明石・姫路 ·················· 14

obe City　神戸市 ·················· 16
Central Kōbe　神戸市中心部 ·················· 18

saka City　大阪市 ·················· 20
Central Ōsaka (1)
大阪市中心部(1) ·················· 22
Central Ōsaka(2)
大阪市中心部(2) ·················· 24
Central Ōsaka(3)
大阪市中心部(3) ·················· 26

yōto & Vicinity
京都とその周辺 ·················· 28
yōto City　京都市 ·················· 30
Central Kyōto(1)
京都市中心部(1) ·················· 32
Central Kyōto(2)
京都市中心部(2) ·················· 34
Central Kyōto(3)
京都市中心部(3) ·················· 36

Central Kyōto(4)
京都市中心部(4) ·················· 38
Central Kyōto(5)
京都市中心部(5) ·················· 40
Central Kyōto(6)
京都市中心部(6) ·················· 42
Central Kyōto(7)
京都市中心部(7) ·················· 44

Nara & Vicinity
奈良とその周辺 ·················· 46
Central Nara　奈良市中心部 ·················· 48
Asuka　飛鳥 ·················· 49

Kinki Area Rail System
近畿圏電車路線図 ·················· 50
Keihanshin Nagoya Subway
京阪神・名古屋地下鉄 ·················· 52
Chūkyō (Nagoya) Area
中京(名古屋)圏 ·················· 54
Nagoya City　名古屋市 ·················· 56
Central Nagoya　名古屋市中心部 ·················· 58
Chūkyō (Nagoya) Area Rail System
中京(名古屋)圏電車路線図 ·················· 60

Nanki, Ise-Shima　南紀・伊勢志摩 ·················· 62
Biwako & Vicinity
琵琶湖とその周辺 ·················· 64

INDEXES　索引 ·················· 65
SUPPLEMENS　補遺 ·················· 86

KEY 地域図凡例

ŌSAKA
大阪 — Prefecture 府県

◎ IZUMI 和泉 — City (-shi) 市

⊙ Town (-chō, -machi) 町

○ Village (-son, -mura) 村

⬥—⬥ Prefectural Boundary 府県界

Municipal Boundary 市郡界

Town & Village Boundary 町村界

J. R. Line JR線

Bullet train line (shinkansen) 新幹線

Other Railway その他の鉄道

Ropeway ロープウェイ

Expressway 高速道路
Toll Road 有料道路

National Road 国道

Other Road その他の道路

Ferry 航路

National Park 国立公園

Guasi National Park 国定公園

▲ Mountaintop 山頂

∴ Tourist spot or Place of Historic Interest 名所旧跡

♨ Hot Spring (Spa) 温泉

Ħ Shinto Shrine (-Jinja, -gū) 神社

卍 Buddhist Temple (-ji, -in, -an) 寺院

✝ Church, Cathedral 教会

⚐ Golf Course ゴルフ場

✿ Factory 工場

⚓ Harbor 港湾

⚲ Lighthouse 灯台

✈ Airport 空港

City Maps 市街図

◎ City Office 市役所　　⊗ Police Station 警察署
○ Ward Office 区役所　　〒 Post Office 郵便局
♁ Government Office 官公庁　⊞ Hospital 病院
　 Embassy 外国公館　　　✕ School 学校

Subway 地下鉄　　　　Ward Boundary 区界

2

A

山陰海岸国立公園
SAN-IN KAIGAN N.P.
TOYOOKA 豊岡
Onsen 温泉
HYOGO 兵庫
CHUGOKU 中国自動
TATSUNO 竜野
AIOI 相生
HIMEJI 姫路
KASAI 加西
TAKASAGO 高砂
KAKOGA KAKOGAWA
Harima Nada 播磨灘
SETONAIKAI NAT'L PARK 瀬戸内海国立公園
Awajishima 淡路島
SUMOTO 洲本
NARUTO-OHASHI 鳴門大橋
NARUTO 鳴門
TOKUSHIMA AIRPORT 徳島空港
Yoshino-gawa 吉野川
TOKUSHIMA 徳島
KOMATSUSHIMA 小松島
ANAN 阿南
TOKUSHIMA 徳島
Kii Sendo 紀伊水道

62

Kinki Area
近畿地方

A

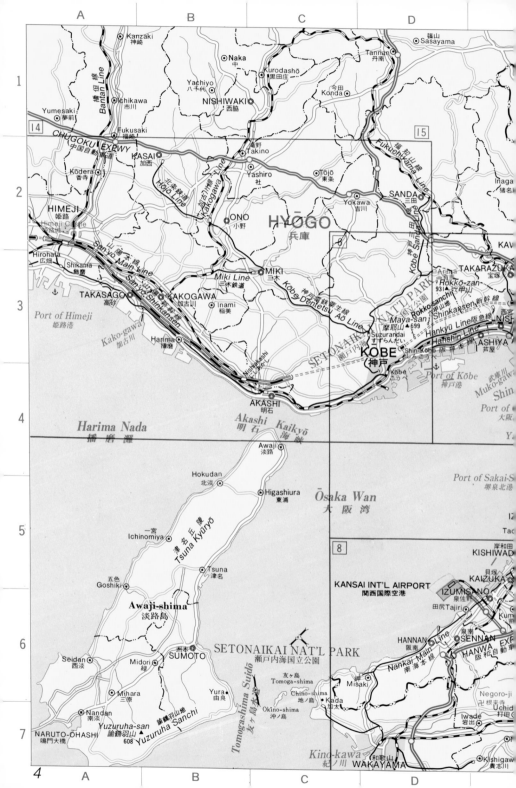

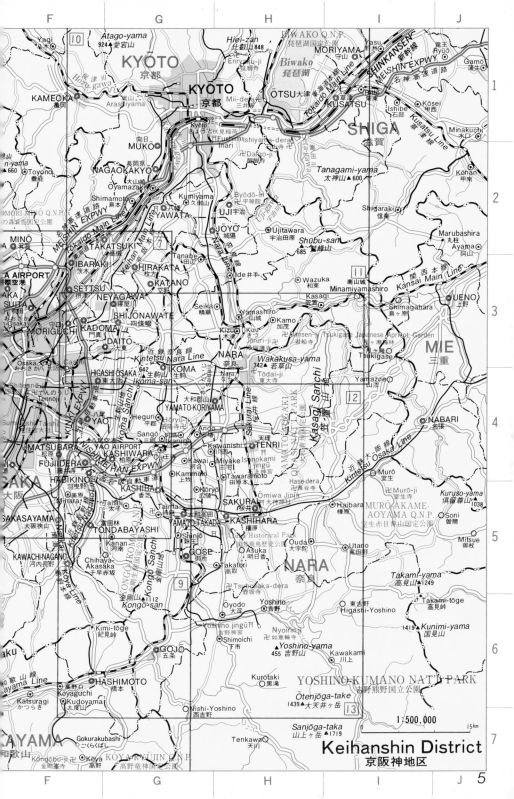

Keihanshin District
京阪神地区

1:500,000

0   15km

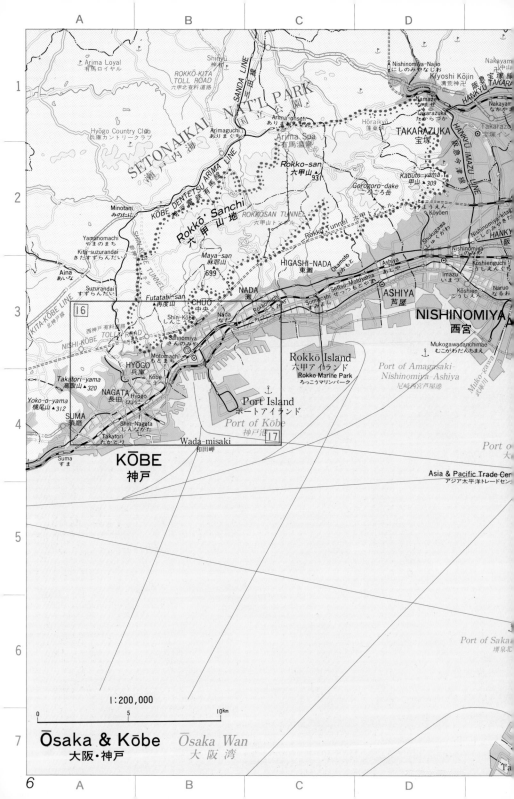

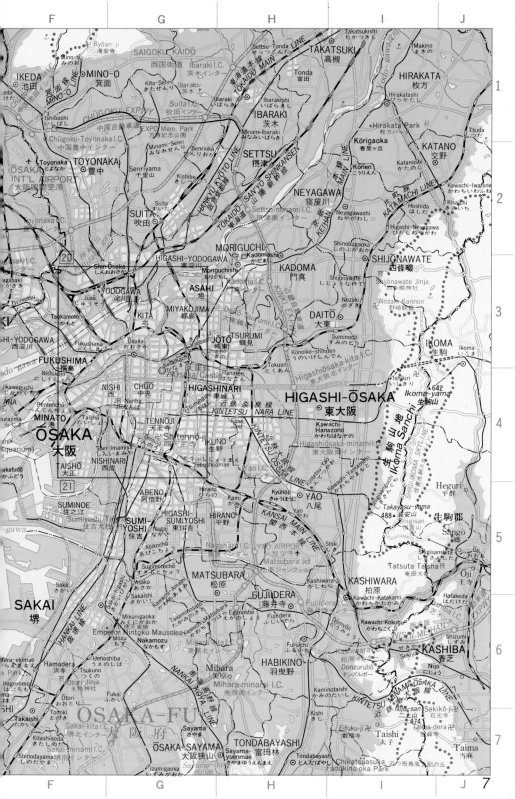

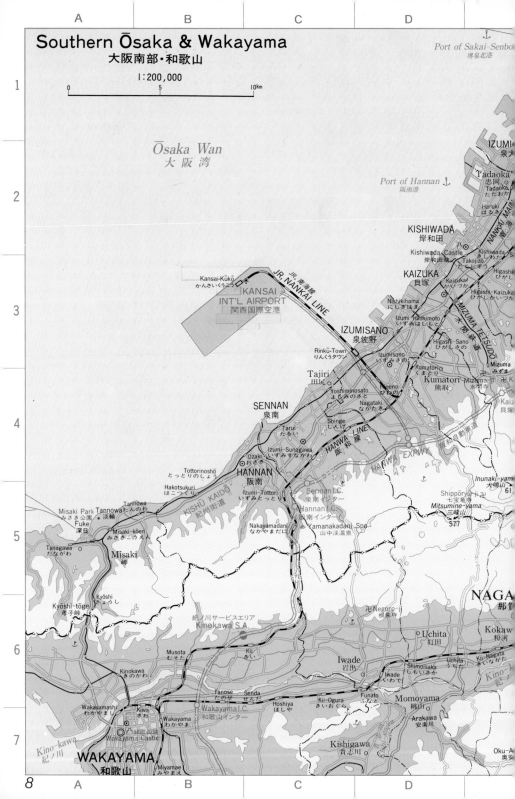

Southern Ōsaka & Wakayama
大阪南部・和歌山

1:200,000

Ōsaka Wan
大阪湾

Port of Sakai-Senbo
堺泉北港

IZUMI
泉大

Tadaoka
忠岡
Tadaoka
ただおか

Port of Hannan
阪南港

Haruki
はるき

KISHIWADA
岸和田

Kishiwada Castle
岸和田城

Kishiwada
きしわだ

Takojizo
たこじぞう

Higashi
ひがし

KAIZUKA
貝塚

Kaizuka
かいづか

Higashi-Kaizuka
ひがしかいづか

Kansai-Kūkō
かんさいくうこう

JR NANKAI LINE
JR 南海線

Nishikihama
にしきはま

Izumi Hashimoto
いずみはしもと

KANSAI
INT'L AIRPORT
関西国際空港

IZUMISANO
泉佐野

Higashi-Sano
ひがしさの

Mizuma
みずま

Rinkū-Town
りんくうタウン

Izumisano
いずさきの

Kumatori
くまとり

Mizuma
みずま

Tajiri
田尻

Kumatori
熊取

Kaiz
貝塚

Yoshiminosato
よしみのさと

Hineno
ひねの

Nagataki
なかたき

SENNAN
泉南

Shinge
しんげ

HANWA LINE
阪和線

Tarui
たるい

Izumi-Sunagawa
いずみすなかわ

HANWA EXPRWY

Tottorinoshō
とっとりのしょう

Ozaki
おざき

Izumi-Tottori
いずみととり

Inunaki-yam
犬鳴山 61

HANNAN
阪南

Sennan I.C.
泉南インター

Shippōryu-ji
七宝竜寺

Hakotsukuri
はこつくり

Hannan I.C.
阪南インター

Mitsumine-yama
三峰山 577

Tannowa
たんのわ

Nakayamadani
なかやまだに

Yamanakadani Spa
山中渓温泉

Misaki Park
みさき公園

Tannowa
淡輪

Fuke
深日

Misaki-kōen
みさきこうえん

KISHŪ KAIDŌ
紀州街道

NAGA
那賀

Tanagawa
たながわ

Misaki
岬

Negoro-ji
根来寺

Kyōshi-tōge
孝子峠

Kyōshi
きょうし

Kinokawa S.A.
紀ノ川サービスエリア

Uchita
打田

Kokaw
粉河

Kii
きい

Iwade
岩出

Musota
むそた

Shimoisaka
しもいさか

Kii-Nagata
きいながた

Iwade
いわで

Kino-
紀ノ

Kinokawa
きのかわ

Tanose
たのせ

Senda
せんだ

Kii-Ogura
きいおくら

Funato
ふなと

Momoyama
桃山

Wakayamashi
わかやまし

Kiwa
きわ

Hoshiya
ほしや

Arakawa
安楽川

Wakayama I.C.
和歌山インター

Wakayama
わかやま

Kishigawa
貴志川

Oku-A
奥

WAKAYAMA
和歌山

Miyamae
みやまえ

Wakayama Castle

Kino-kawa
紀ノ川

8

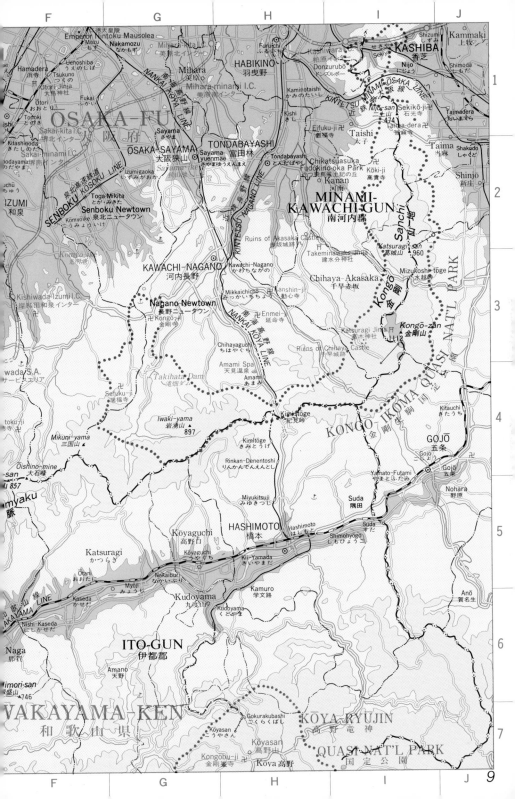

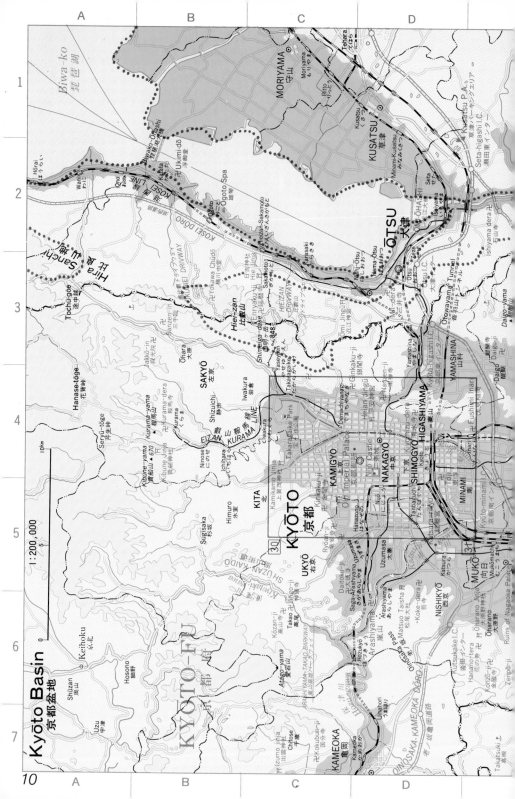

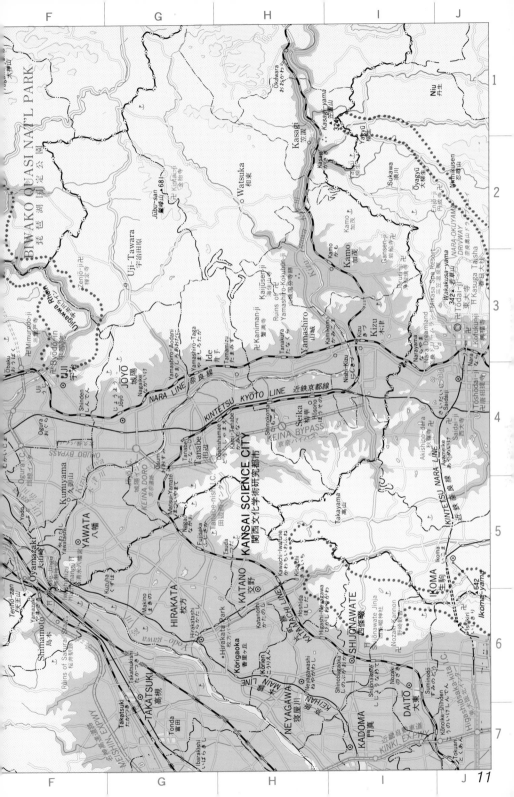

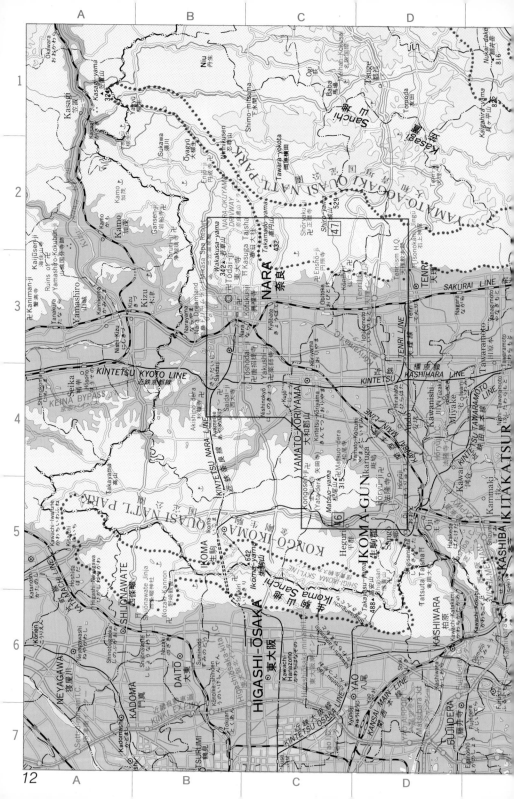

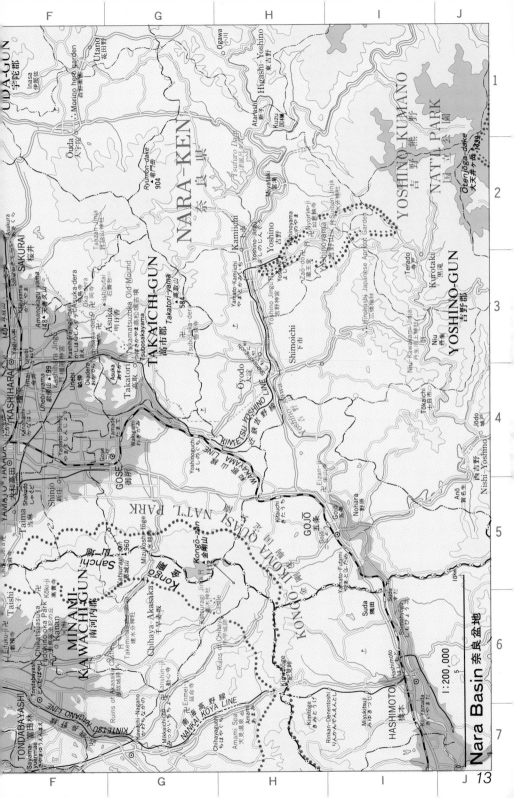

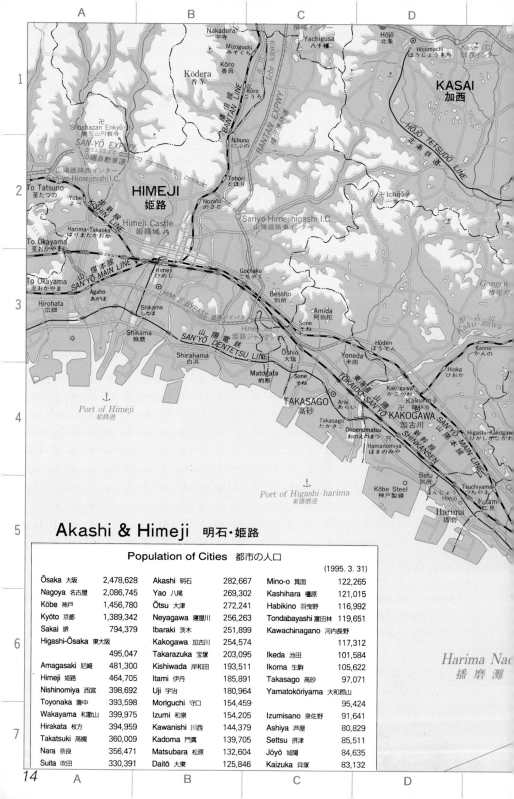

Akashi & Himeji 明石・姫路

Population of Cities 都市の人口

(1995. 3. 31)

City		Population	City		Population	City		Population
Ōsaka	大阪	2,478,628	Akashi	明石	282,667	Mino-o	箕面	122,265
Nagoya	名古屋	2,086,745	Yao	八尾	269,302	Kashihara	橿原	121,015
Kōbe	神戸	1,456,780	Ōtsu	大津	272,241	Habikino	羽曳野	116,992
Kyōto	京都	1,389,342	Neyagawa	寝屋川	256,263	Tondabayashi	富田林	119,651
Sakai	堺	794,379	Ibaraki	茨木	251,899	Kawachinagano	河内長野	117,312
Higashi-Ōsaka	東大阪	495,047	Kakogawa	加古川	254,574			
Amagasaki	尼崎	481,300	Takarazuka	宝塚	203,095	Ikeda	池田	101,584
Himeji	姫路	464,705	Kishiwada	岸和田	193,511	Ikoma	生駒	105,622
Nishinomiya	西宮	398,692	Itami	伊丹	185,891	Takasago	高砂	97,071
Toyonaka	豊中	393,598	Uji	宇治	180,964	Yamatokōriyama	大和郡山	95,424
Wakayama	和歌山	399,975	Moriguchi	守口	154,489	Izumisano	泉佐野	91,641
Hirakata	枚方	394,959	Izumi	和泉	154,205	Ashiya	芦屋	80,829
Takatsuki	高槻	360,009	Kawanishi	川西	144,379	Settsu	摂津	85,511
Nara	奈良	356,471	Kadoma	門真	139,705	Jōyō	城陽	84,635
Suita	吹田	330,391	Matsubara	松原	132,604	Kaizuka	貝塚	83,132
			Daitō	大東	125,846			

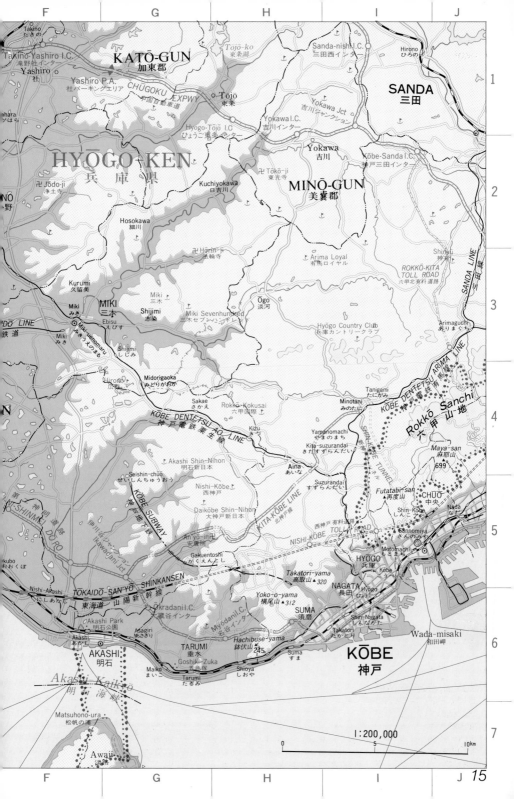

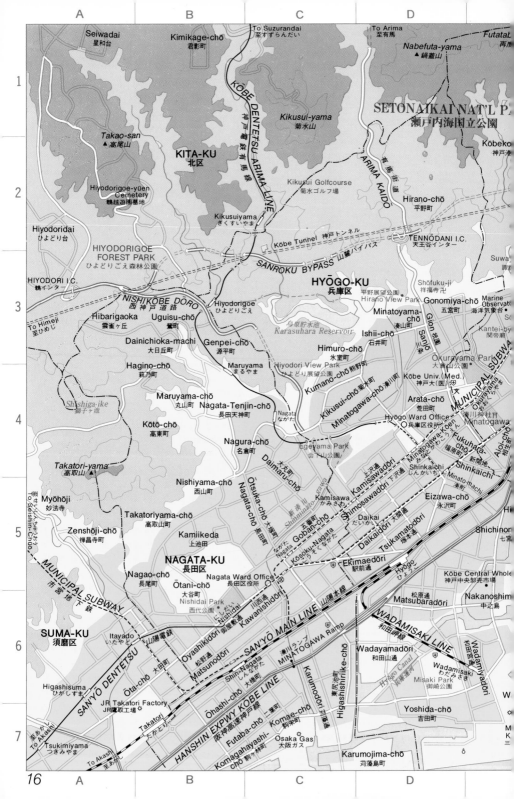

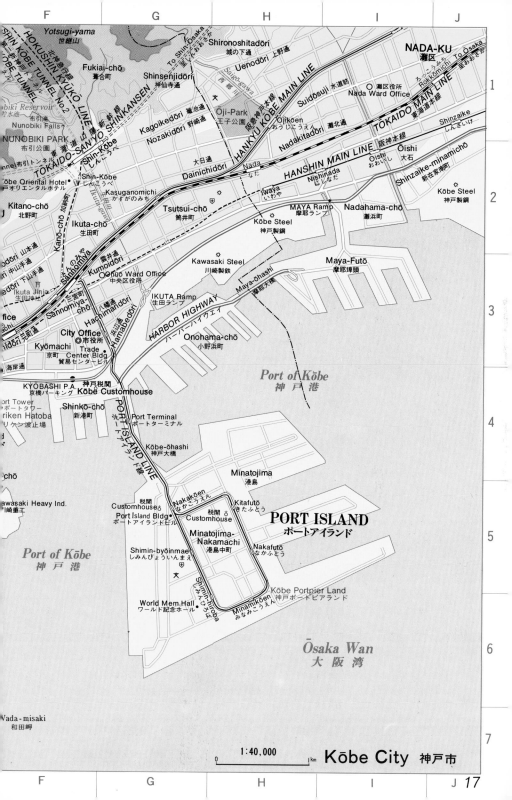

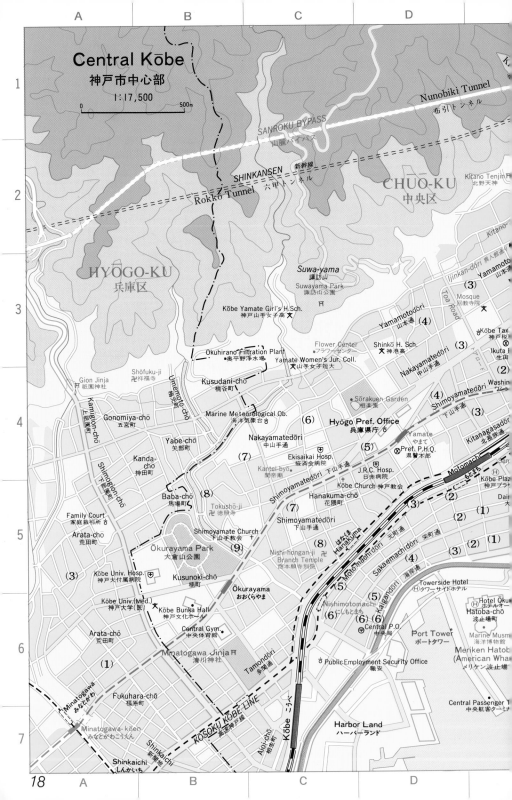

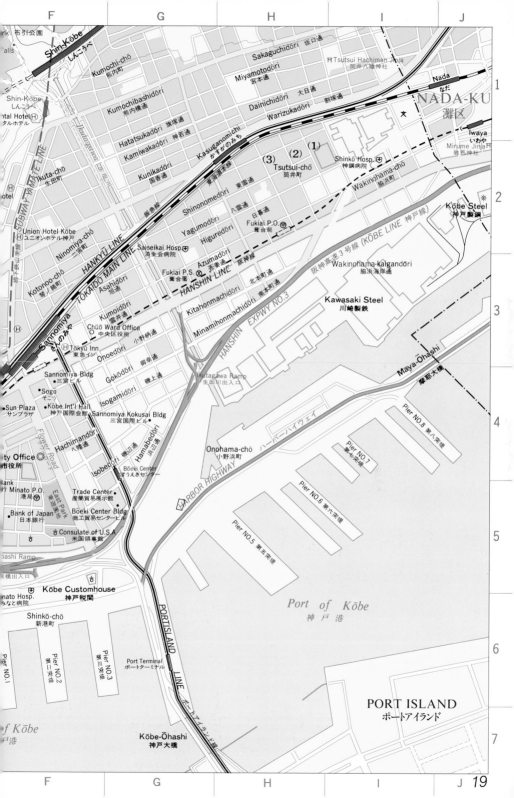

F	G	H	I	J	

Shin-Kōbe
しんこうべ

布引公園

Shin-Kōbe
しんこうべ

タルホテル

Kumochi-chō
熊内町

Sakaguchidōri 坂口通

Tsutsui Hachiman Jinja
筒井八幡神社

NADA-KU
灘区

Nada
なだ

Miyamotodōri
宮本通

Kumochibashidōri
熊内橋通

Hatatsukadōri 旗塚通

Kamiwakadōri 神若通

Dainichidōri 大日通

Warizukadōri 割塚通

Iwaya
いわや

Mirume Jinja
敏馬神社

Union Hotel Kōbe
ユニオンホテル神戸

Kunikadōri
国香通

Kasuganomichi
かすがのみち

(3)   (2) (1)

Tsutsui-chō
筒井町

Shinkō Hosp.
神鋼病院

Wakinohama-chō
脇浜町

Kōbe Steel
神戸製鋼

Shinonomedōri
東雲通

Yagumodōri
八雲通

Higuredōri
日暮通

Fukiai P.O.
葺合局

Ninomiya-chō
二宮町

Kotonoo-chō
琴ノ緒町

Saiseikai Hosp.
済生会病院

Fukiai P.S.
葺合署

Azumadōri
吾妻通

Wakinohama-kaigandōri
脇浜海岸通

KOBE LINE 神戸線

阪神高速3号線 (KOBE LINE 神戸線)

Asahidōri
旭通

Kimoidōri
雲井通

Chūō Ward Office
中央区役所

Kitahonmachidōri
北本町通

Minamihonmachidōri
南本町通

Kawasaki Steel
川崎製鉄

HANSHIN EXPWY NO.3

Tōkyū Inn
東急イン

Onoedōri
王子公園通

Gokōdōri
御幸通

Isogamidōri
磯上通

Ikutagawa Ramp
生田川入口

Maya-Ōhashi
摩耶大橋

Sannomiya Bldg
三宮ビル

Sogo
そごう

Sun Plaza
サンプラザ

Kōbe Int'l Hall
神戸国際会館

Sannomiya Kokusai Bldg
三宮国際ビル

Hachimandōri
八幡通

Isobedōri
磯辺通

Hamabedōri
浜辺通

Onohama-chō
小野浜町

Pier NO.8 第八突堤

Pier NO.7 第七突堤

ity Office
市役所

Minato P.O.
港局

Trade Center
産業貿易展示館

Bōeki Center
ぼうえきセンター

HARBOR HIGHWAY

HARBOR HIGHWAY

Pier NO.6 第六突堤

Bank

Bank of Japan
日本銀行

Bōeki Center Bldg
商工貿易センタービル

Consulate of U.S.A
米国領事館

Pier NO.5 第五突堤

Port of Kōbe
神戸港

ōhashi Ramp

Kōbe Customhouse
神戸税関

inato Hosp.
みなと病院

Shinkō-chō
新港町

PORT ISLAND LINE ポートアイランド線

Pier NO.1

Pier NO.2 第二突堤

Pier NO.3 第三突堤

Port Terminal
ポートターミナル

PORT ISLAND
ポートアイランド

f Kōbe
戸港

Kōbe-Ōhashi
神戸大橋

F	G	H	I	J	*19*

SUBWAY YAMATE LINE

HANKYU LINE

TOKAIDO MAIN LINE

HANSHIN LINE

Flower Road

East Park

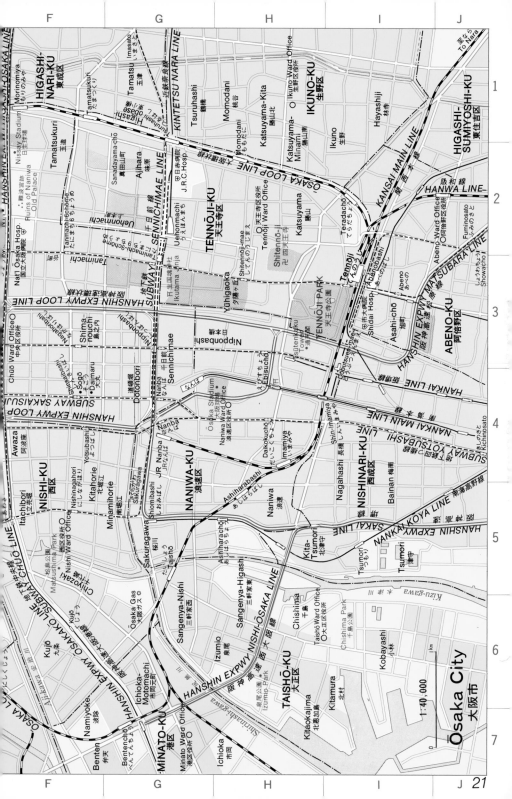

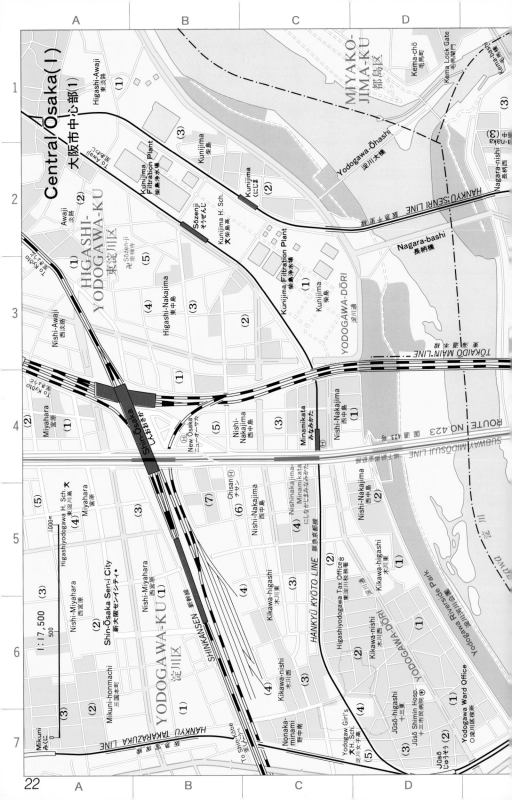

MIYAKO-
JIMA-KU
都島区

Kema Lock Gate
毛馬閘門

Kema-chō
毛馬町

Kema-bashi
毛馬橋

Higashi-Awaji
東淡路 (1)

(3)

(1)

(3)

Awaji
淡路 (2)

HIGASHI-
YODOGAWA-KU
東淀川区

Kunijima
Filtration Plant
柴島浄水場

Kunijima
柴島

Sōzenji
そうぜんじ
卍崇禅寺

Kunijima H. Sch.
柴島高

Kunijima
くにじま (2)

Kunijima Filtration Plant
柴島浄水場

Yodogawa-Ōhashi
淀川大橋

Nagara-nishi
長柄西

Nagara-bashi
長柄橋

a-naka(3)
中(3)

(1)

(5)

Higashi-Nakajima
東中島 (3)

(2)

Kunijima
柴島 (1)

YODOGAWA-DŌRI
淀川通

HANKYŪ SENRI LINE

To Kyōto (1)

Nishi-Awaji
西淡路

(4)

(1)

TŌKAIDŌ MAIN LINE

To Kyōto (2)

Miyahara
宮原 (1)

Shin-Ōsaka
しんおおさか

New Ōsaka
ニューオーサカ

(5)

Nishi-
Nakajima
西中島 (3)

Minamikata
みなみかた

Nishi-Nakajima
西中島 (1)

ROUTE NO.423
国道423号

SUBWAY MIDŌSUJI LINE
地下鉄御堂筋線

(5)

Higashiyodogawa H. Sch.
東淀川高

Miyahara
宮原 (4)

(3)

Chisan
チサン (H)

Nishinakajima-
Minamikata
にしなかじまみなみかた

Nishi-Nakajima
西中島 (4)

Nishi-Nakajima
西中島 (2)

1000m

(7)

(6)

Nishi-Miyahara
西宮原

Shin-Ōsaka Sen-i City
新大阪センイシティ

Nishi-Miyahara
西宮原 (1)

(4)

Kikawa-higashi
木川東 (3)

(2)

Kikawa-higashi
木川東

Yodogawa Riverside Park
淀川河川公園

1:17,500

500

(3)

Nishi-Miyahara
西宮原 (2)

YODOGAWA-KU
淀川区

SHINKANSEN
新幹線

HANKYŪ KYŌTO LINE
阪急京都線

Higashiyodogawa Tax Office
東淀川税務署 (8)

Kikawa-nishi
木川西

(4)

(2)

YODOGAWA-DŌRI
淀川通

(1)

Mikuni-honmachi
三国本町

(2)

Kikawa-nishi
木川西 (4)

淀川西

Kikawa-nishi
木川西 (3)

(2)

Mikuni
みくに (3)

(1)

Nonaka-
minami
野中南 (1)

Yodogawa Girl's
H. Sch.
淀川女子高

Jūsō-higashi
十三東 (4)

Jūsō Shimin Hosp.
十三市民病院 (H)

Jūsō
じゅうそう (2)

Yodogawa Ward Office
淀川区役所

To Takarazuka
宝塚へ

HANKYŪ TAKARAZUKA LINE
阪急宝塚線

To Shin-Kōbe
新神戸へ

(5)

(3)

淀川
D0川

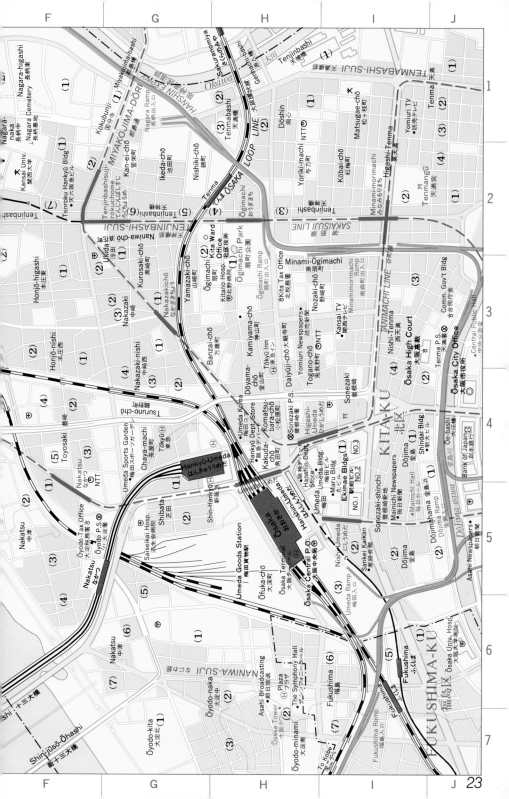

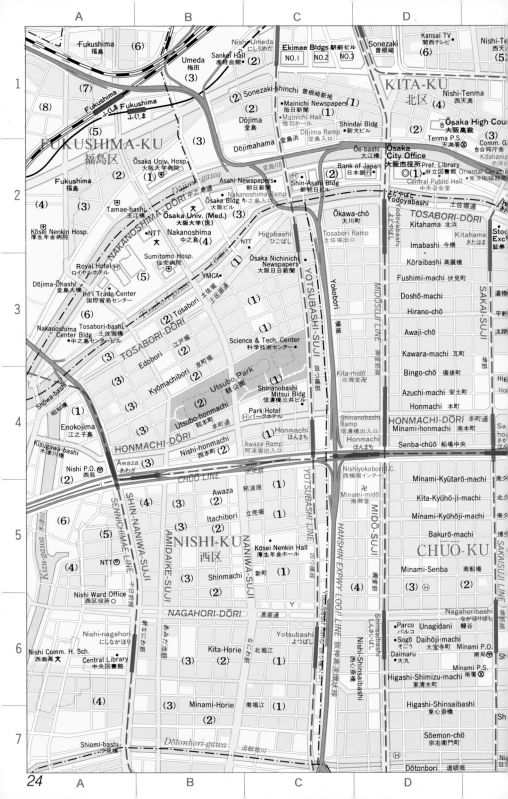

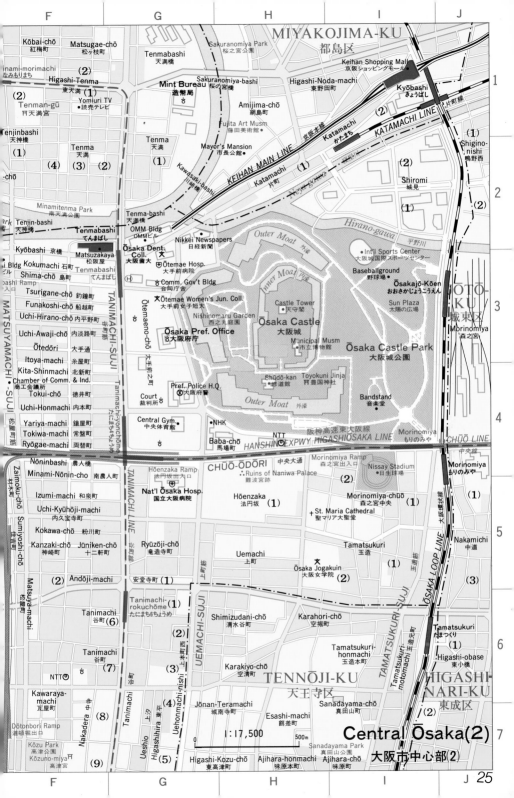

Central Ōsaka(2)
大阪市中心部(2)

1:17,500

25

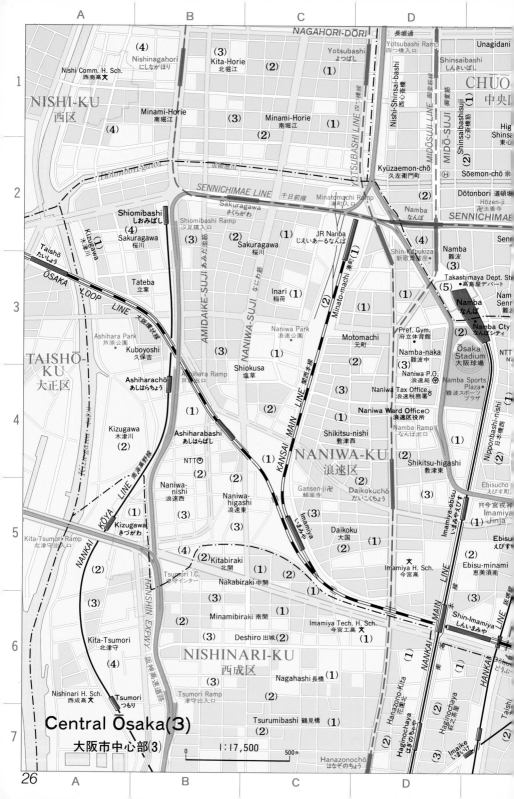

NAGAHORI-DŌRI

長堀通

Unagidani

Yotsubashi Ramp
四つ橋入口

Shinsaibashi
しんさいばし

Yotsubashi
よつばし

CHŪŌ
中央区

(4)

Nishi Comm. H. Sch.
西商高

Nishinagahori
にしながほり

Kita-Horie
北堀江

(3)

(2)

(1)

Shinsaibashisuji
心斎橋筋

Hig
Shinsa
東心

NISHI-KU
西区

(4)

Minami-Horie
南堀江

(3)

Minami-Horie
南堀江

(1)

Nishi-Shinsai-bashi
西心斎橋

MIDŌ-SUJI LINE
御堂筋線

MIDŌ-SUJI

(4)

(2)

Sōemon-chō 宗

Dōtonbori 道頓堀

Hōzen-ji 法善寺

2

Dōtonbori-gawa

道頓堀川

SENNICHIMAE LINE

千日前線

Kyūzaemon-chō
久左衛門町

(2)

Namba
なんば

SENNICHIMAE

Sakuragawa
さくらがわ

Minatomachi Ramp
湊町入口

Shiomibashi
しおみばし

(4)

Shiomibashi Ramp
汐見橋入口

(3)

(2)

Sakuragawa
桜川

(1)

JR Nanba
じぇいあーるなんば

(3)

Shin-Kabukiza
新歌舞伎座

Namba
難波

Sen

Taishō
たいしょう

(1)

Sakuragawa
桜川

(1)

(1)

Takashimaya Dept. Sto.
高島屋デパート

(5)

Nam
Senr

Kizugawa
木津川

Tateba
立葉

Inari (1)
稲荷

Namba
なんば

Nam

OSAKA LOOP LINE

大阪環状線

Naniwa Park
浪速公園

(1)

Pref. Gym.
府立体育館

Namba City
なんばシティ

3

TAISHŌ-KU
大正区

Ashihara Park
芦原公園

Kuboyoshi
久保吉

(3)

Shiokusa
塩草

Motomachi
元町

Namba-naka
難波中

(2)

Ōsaka Stadium
大阪球場

Naniwa P.O.
浪速郵便局

Namba Sports Plaza
難波スポーツプラザ

NTT

Ashiharachō
あしはらちょう

Ashihara Ramp
芦原出口

(1)

(3)

Naniwa Tax Office
浪速税務署

(1)

Ashiharabashi
あしはらばし

(1)

Shikitsu-nishi
敷津西

Naniwa Ward Office
浪速区役所

(1)

NTT

(2)

(1)

(3)

Namba Ramp
なんば出口

Shikitsu-higashi
敷津東

Nipponbashi-nishi
日本橋西

(2)

NANIWA-KU
浪速区

Naniwa-nishi
浪速西

Gansen-ji 顔泉寺

Daikokuchō
だいこくちょう

(3)

Ebisucho
えびす町

4

Kizugawa
木津川

(2)

Naniwa-higashi
浪速東

(3)

Daikoku
大国

(2)

Imamiya-ebisu
いまみやえびす

Imamiya Jinja
今宮戎神社

Ebisu
えびす

KŌYA LINE 南海高野線

(1)

Kizugawa
きづがわ

(3)

(1)

Imamiya H. Sch.
今宮高

(2)

Ebisu-minami
恵美須南

5

Kita-Tsumori Ramp
北津守出口

NANKAI

(4)

Kitabiraki
北開

(2)

Ebisu
えびす

(2)

Nakabiraki 中開

HANSHIN EXPWY 阪神高速道路

(2)

Tsumori I.C.
津守インター

(1)

Imamiya Tech. H. Sch.
今宮工高

Shin-Imamiya
しんいまみや

(2)

(3)

Minamibiraki 南開

(1)

(3)

NANKAI MAIN LINE 南海本線

(3)

6

Kita-Tsumori
北津守

(4)

(3)

Deshiro 出城

(2)

(1)

NISHINARI-KU
西成区

Nagahashi 長橋

(1)

Hanazono-Kita
花園北

(2)

Haginochaya
萩之茶屋

Imaike
いまいけ

Nishinari H. Sch.
西成高

Tsumori
つもり

Tsumori Ramp
津守出口

(3)

(2)

(2)

Central Ōsaka(3)
大阪市中心部(3)

Tsurumibashi 鶴見橋

(1)

Haginochaya
はぎのちゃや

(2)

HANKAI

1:17,500

0   500 m

Hanazonochō
はなぞのちょう

7

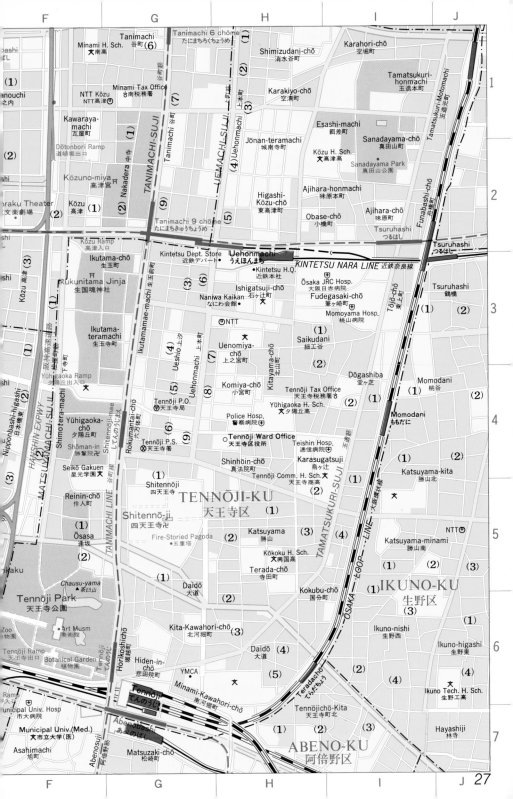

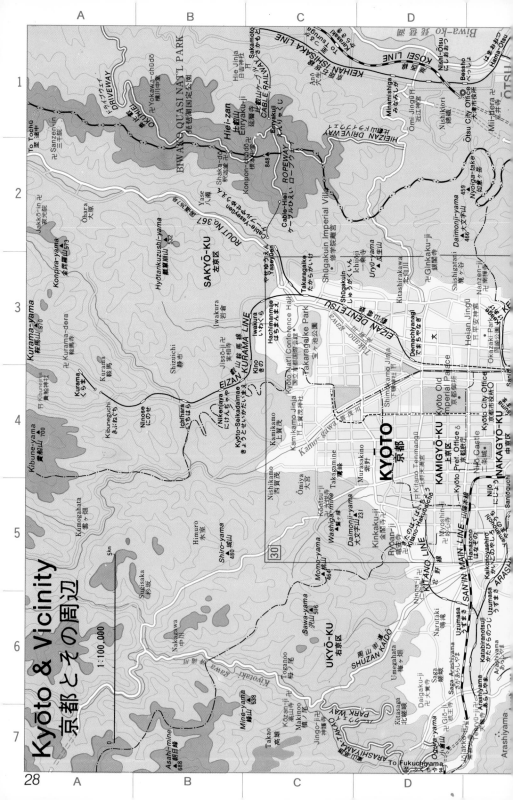

Kyōto & Vicinity
京都とその周辺

1:100,000

5Km
0

A   B   C   D

KYOTO
京都

SAKYŌ-KU
左京区

KAMIGYŌ-KU
上京区

NAKAGYŌ-KU
中京区

UKYŌ-KU
右京区

SHUZAN-KU

Hiei-zan
比叡山

BIWAKO QUASI NAT'L PARK
琵琶湖国定公園

ŌKUHIEI DRIVEWAY

Kurama-yama
鞍馬山 570

Kibune-yama
貴船山 700

Konpira-yama
金毘羅山 573

Hyōtankuzushi-yama
瓢箪崩山 532

Daimonji-yama
大文字山 466

Takaragaike Park
宝ヶ池公園

Kyōto Nat'l Conference Hall
国立京都国際会館

HIEIZAN DRIVEWAY

KOSEI LINE

KEIHAN ISHIYAMA LINE

CABLE RAILWAY

ROPEWAY ロープウェイ

ROUTE No.367

EIZAN KURAMA LINE

EIZAN DENTETSU

KITANO LINE

SAN-IN MAIN LINE

SAN-IN LINE

ARASHIYAMA PARK WAY

To Fukuchiyama

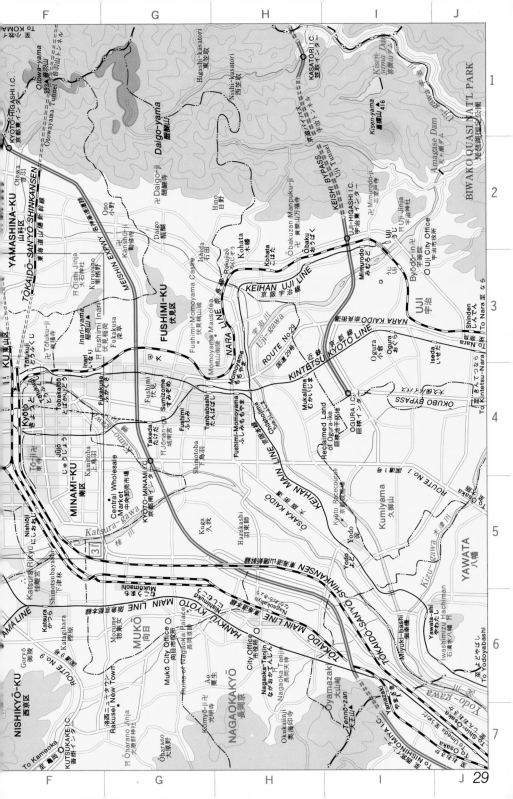

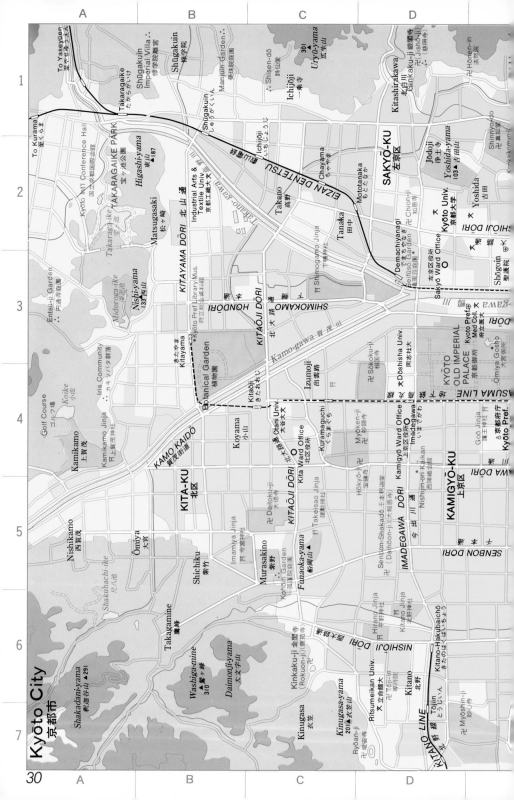

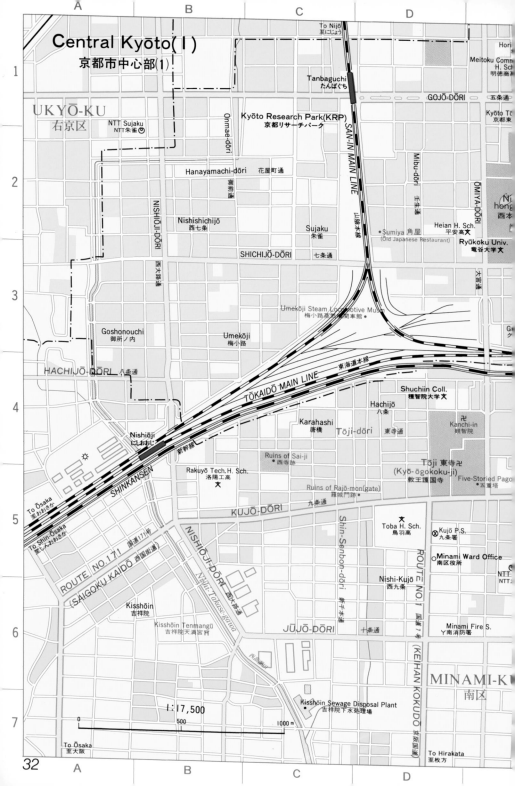

Central Kyōto(1)
京都市中心部(1)

UKYŌ-KU
右京区

To Nijō
至にじょう

Tanbaguchi
たんばぐち

GOJŌ-DŌRI 五条通

Kyōto Research Park(KRP)
京都リサーチパーク

Meitoku Comm.
H. Sch.
明徳商業

Kyōto Tō
京都東

NTT Sujaku
NTT朱雀

Onmae-dori 御前通

Hanayamachi-dōri 花屋町通

Mibu-dōri 壬生通

ŌMIYA-DŌRI 大宮通

hong
西本

NISHIŌJI-DŌRI 西大路通

Nishishichijō
西七条

Sujaku
朱雀

SHICHIJŌ-DŌRI 七条通

Sumiya 角屋
(Old Japanese Restaurant)

Heian H. Sch.
平安高

Ryūkoku Univ.
龍谷大学

SAN-IN MAIN LINE 山陰本線

Ōmiya-dōri 大宮通

Umekōji Steam Locomotive Mus.
梅小路蒸気機関車館

G

Goshonouchi
御所ノ内

Umekōji
梅小路

HACHIJŌ-DŌRI 八条通

TŌKAIDŌ MAIN LINE 東海道本線

Shuchiin Coll.
種智院大学

Hachijō
八条

Kanchi-in
観智院

Karahashi
唐橋

Tōji-dōri 東寺通

Tōji 東寺
(Kyō-ōgokoku-ji)
教王護国寺

Nishiōji
にしおおじ

SHINKANSEN 新幹線

Rakuyō Tech. H. Sch.
洛陽工高

Ruins of Sai-ji
西寺跡

Ruins of Rajō-mon(gate)
羅城門跡

Five-Storied Pago
五重塔

To Ōsaka
至おおさか

To Shin-Ōsaka
至しんおおさか

KUJŌ-DŌRI 九条通

Shin-Senbon-dōri 新千本通

Toba H. Sch.
鳥羽高

Kujō P.S.
九条署

Minami Ward Office
南区役所

NTT.
NTT.

ROUTE NO.171 国道171号

(SAIGOKU KAIDŌ) 西国街道

NISHIŌJI-DŌRI 西大路通

Nishi-Takase-kaidō 新千本通

Nishi-Kujō
西九条

ROUTE NO.1 国道1号

Kisshōin
吉祥院

Kisshōin Tenmangū
吉祥院天満宮

JŪJŌ-DŌRI 十条通

Minami Fire S.
南消防署

MINAMI-KU
南区

(KEIHAN KOKUDŌ) 京阪国道

1:17,500

0   500   1000 m

Kisshōin Sewage Disposal Plant
吉祥院下水処理場

To Ōsaka
至大阪

To Hirakata
至枚方

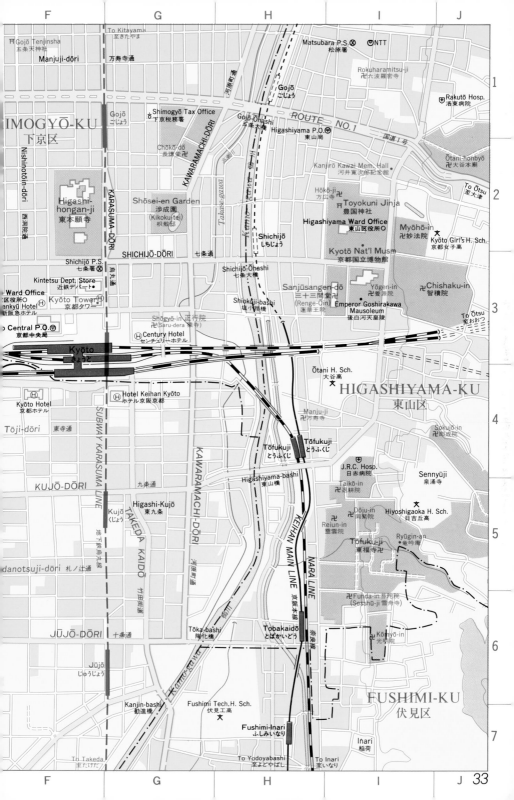

Central Kyōto(2)
京都市中心部(2)

1 : 17,500

0　　　　500　　　　1000 m

Nakadachūri-dōri

Ninnaji-dōri　仁和寺通

Jōfukuji-dōri　浄福寺通

Shichihonmatsu-dōri　七本松通

Onmae-dōri　御前通

Tenjin-dōri　天神通

Chikurin-ji　竹林寺卍

SENBON-DŌRI

Kannon-ji　観音寺卍

Ruins of Heia　平安宮内

Social Education Center　社会教育センター

Sawar

Hōrin-ji　法輪寺卍
(Daruma-dera)　だるま寺

MARUTAMACHI-DŌRI　丸太町通

To Hanazono　至はなぞの

NISHIŌJI-DŌRI　西大路通

NHK Kyōto　NHK京都

Nijō Park　二条公園

Hanazono Univ.　花園大学 ✕

Rakuyō Girls H. Sch.　洛陽女子高 ✕

天神川

Tenjin-gawa

Meteorological Observatory　地方気象台

Suzaku Park　朱雀公園

Suzaku H. Sch.　朱雀高 ✕

Nishinokyō　西ノ京

Nijō　にじょう

OIKE-DŌRI　御池通

NAKAG　中京

KEIFUKU ARASHIYAMA LINE

Sanjō-dōri　三条通

SAN-IN MAIN LINE

Yamanouchi　やまのうち

京福嵐山線
Ukyō Tax Office　右京税務署

Sanjōguchi　さんじょうぐち

Kyōto Ryōyō H. Sch.　京都両洋高 ✕

UKYŌ-KU　右京区

Saiin　西院

Saiin-Kasuga Jinja　西院春日神社

Kōsan-ji　高山寺

Rehabilitation Center　リハビリテーションセンター

Shichihonmatsu-dōri　七本松通

SHIJŌ-DŌRI　四条

Saiin　さいいん
山陰本線

Saiin　さいいん
Saiin　さいいん

Mibu　壬生

Mibu-dera　壬生寺卍

Nishikōji　西小路

Takatsuji-dōri　高辻通

HANKYŪ KYŌTO LINE
阪急京都線

To Umeda　至うめだ

Matsubara-dōri　松原通

Municipal Hosp.　市立病院

Tanbaguchi　たんばぐち

GOJŌ-DŌRI　五条通

Kyōto Research Park (KRP)　京都リサーチパーク

To Kyōto　至きょうと

SH

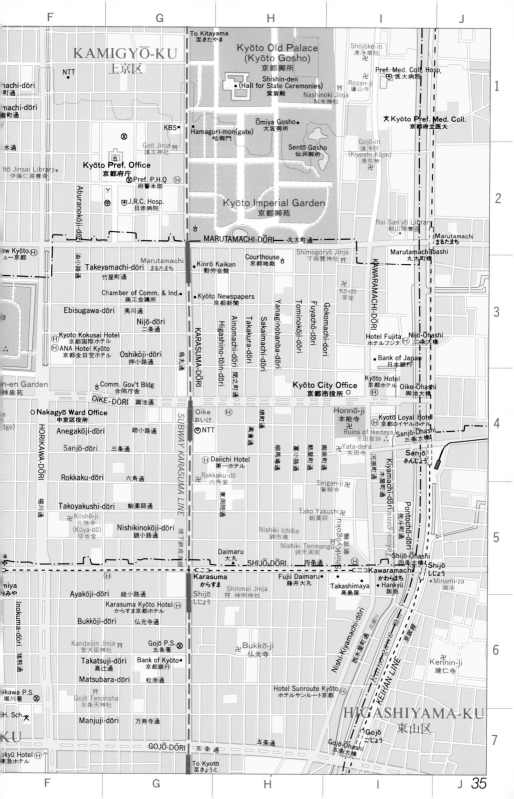

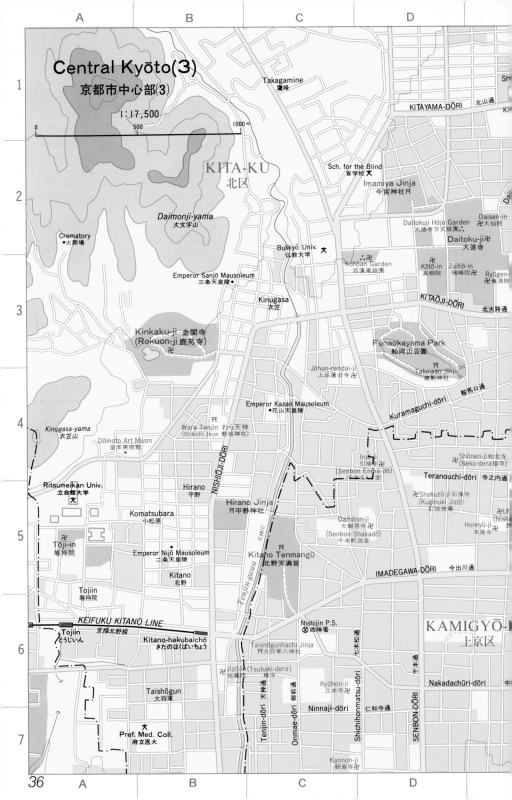

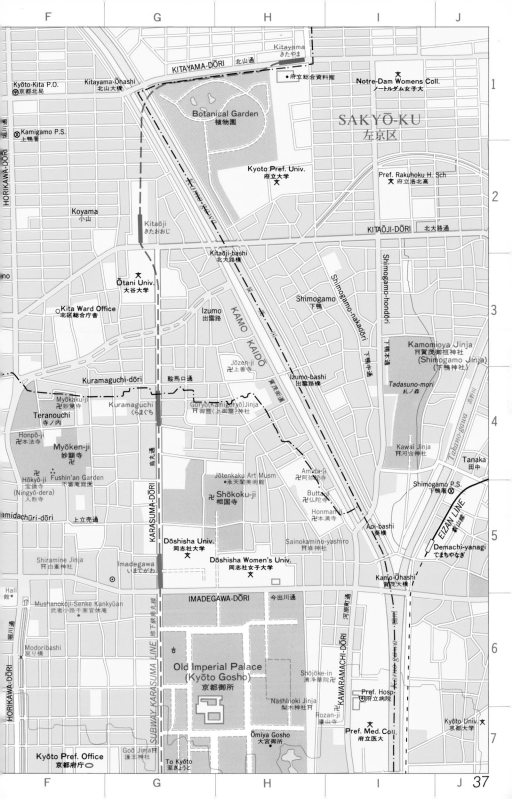

KITAYAMA-DŌRI 北山通

Kitayama
きたやま

1

Kyōto-Kita P.O.
京都北局

Kitayama-Ōhashi
北山大橋

府立総合資料館

Notre-Dam Womens Coll.
ノートルダム女子大

Kamigamo P.S.
上鴨署

Botanical Garden
植物園

SAKYŌ-KU
左京区

Koyama
小山

Kyoto Pref. Univ.
府立大学

Pref. Rakuhoku H. Sch
府立洛北高

2

Kitaōji
きたおおじ

KITAŌJI-DŌRI 北大路通

Kitaōji-bashi
北大路橋

Shimogamo-hondōri

Ōtani Univ.
大谷大学

Izumo
出雲路

Shimogamo
下鴨

Shimogamo-nakadōri

3

Kita Ward Office
北区総合庁舎

Kamomioya Jinja
賀茂御祖神社
(Shimogamo Jinja)
(下鴨神社)

KAMO KAIDŌ

下鴨本通

Jōzen-ji
上善寺

Izumo-bashi
出雲路橋

Tadasuno-mori
糺ノ森

Kuramaguchi-dōri
鞍馬口通

Myōkaku-ji
妙覚寺

Kuramaguchi
くらまぐち

Goryō(Kami Goryō) Jinja
御霊(上御霊)神社

Kawai Jinja
河合神社

Tanaka
田中

4

Teranouchi
寺ノ内

Honpō-ji
本法寺

Hōkyō-ji
宝鏡寺
(Ningyō-dera)
人形寺

Myōken-ji
妙顕寺

Fushin'an Garden
不審庵庭園

Jōtenkaku Art Musm
承天閣美術館

Amida-ji
阿弥陀寺

Shimogamo P.S.
下鴨尾

amidachūri-dōri
上立売通

Shōkoku-ji
相国寺

Buttai-ji
仏陀寺

Honman-ji
本満寺

Aoi-bashi
葵橋

EIZAN LINE
叡山線

5

Shiramine Jinja
白峯神社

Dōshisha Univ.
同志社大学

Dōshisha Women's Univ.
同志社女子大学

Sainokamino-yashiro
西賀茂神社

Kamo-Ōhashi
賀茂大橋

Demachi-yanagi
でまちやなぎ

Imadegawa
いまでがわ

IMADEGAWA-DŌRI 今出川通

Hall
館

Modoribashi
戻り橋

Mushanokōji-Senke Kankyūan
武者小路千家官休庵

6

Old Imperial Palace
(Kyōto Gosho)
京都御所

Shōjōke-in
清浄華院

Pref. Hosp.
府立病院

Nashinoki Jinja
梨木神社

Rozan-ji
廬山寺

KAWARAMACHI-DŌRI

Kyōto Univ.
京都大学

7

Kyōto Pref. Office
京都府庁

Goō Jinja
護王神社

Ōmiya Gosho
大宮御所

Pref. Med. Coll.
府立医大

To Kyōto
至きょうと

HORIKAWA-DŌRI 堀川通

KARASUMA-DŌRI 烏丸通

SUBWAY KARASUMA LINE 地下鉄烏丸線

Takano-gawa 高野川

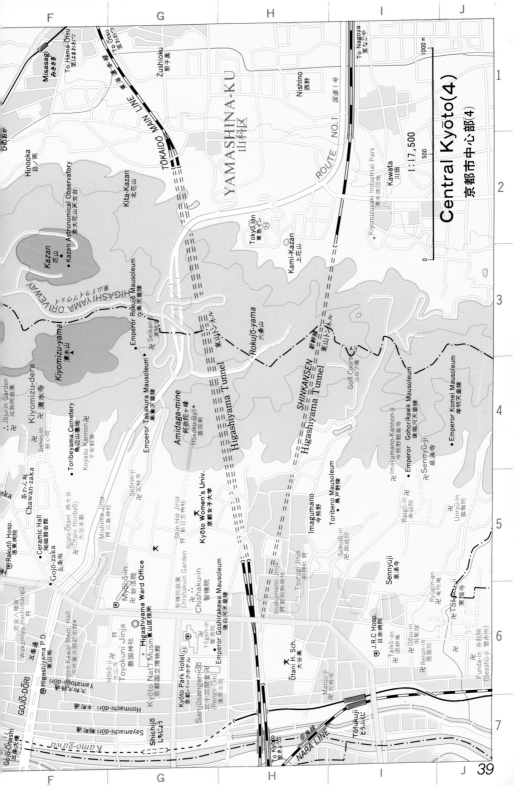

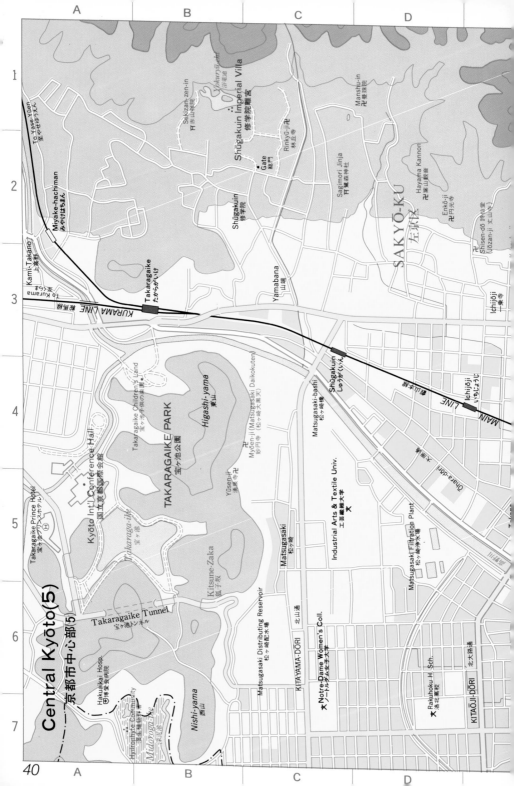

A   B   C   D

1

2

3

4

5

6

7

To Yase-Yūen 八ヶ瀬ゆうえん
Miyake-hachiman みやけはちまん

Kami-Takano 上高野
To Kurama

KURAMA LINE 鞍馬線

Takaragaike たからがいけ

Sekizan-zen-in 卍赤山禅院
Shūgakuin Imperial Villa 修学院離宮
Gate 総門
Rinkyō-ji 卍林丘寺

Manshu-in 卍曼殊院
Hayama Kannon 卍葉山観音

Sagimori Jinja 卍鷺森神社

Enkō-ji 卍円光寺

Shisen-dō 詩仙堂
(Jōzan-ji 丈山寺)

Shūgakuin 卍
Shūgakuin 修学院

SAKYO-KU 左京区

Ichijōji 卍一乗寺

Yamabana 山端

Yamabana 山端

Matsugasaki-bashi 松ヶ崎橋

Shūgakuin しゅうがくいん

Ichijōji いちじょうじ
Ichijōji 卍一乗寺

MAIN LINE 叡山本線

Takaragaike Children's Land 宝ヶ池子供の楽園

Higashi-yama 東山

Myōden-ji (Matsugasaki Daikokuten) 妙顕寺 (松ヶ崎大黒天)

Yūsen-ji 卍湧泉寺

TAKARAGAIKE PARK 宝ヶ池公園

Kyōto Int'l Conference Hall 国立京都国際会館

Takaragaike Prince Hotel 宝ヶ池プリンスホテル Ⓗ

Takaragu-ike 宝ヶ池

Kitsune-Zaka 狐坂

Matsugasaki 松ヶ崎

Industrial Arts & Textile Univ. 工芸繊維大学 🎓

Matsugasaki Filtration Plant 松ヶ崎浄水場

Ohara-dōri

Takaragaike Tunnel 宝ヶ池トンネル

Nishi-yama 西山

Hakuaikai Hosp. 西陣愛会病院

Hydrophytic Community 藻類研究自然群落
Midorogaike 深泥池

Matsugasaki Distributing Reservoir 松ヶ崎配水池

KITAYAMA-DŌRI

北山通 KITAYAMA-DŌRI

🎓Notre-Dame Women's Coll. ノートルダム女子大学

🎓Rakuhoku H. Sch. 洛北高校

北大路通

KITAŌJI-DŌRI

A   B   C   D

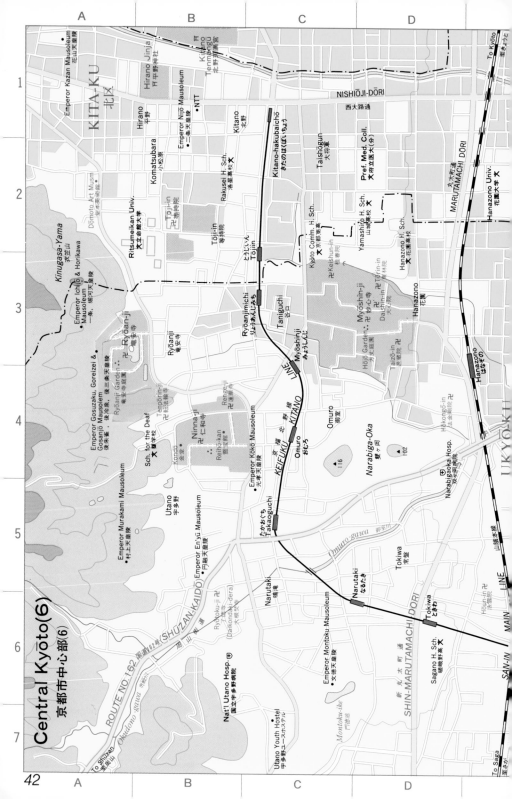

1

Emperor Kazan Mausoleum
花山天皇陵

KITA-KU
北区

Hirano Jinja
平野神社

Kitano
Tenmangū
北野天満宮

NISHIŌJI-DORI
西大路通

To Kyoto
至京都

Emperor Ichijō & Horikawa
一条・堀河天皇陵

Hirano
平野

Emperor Nijō Mausoleum
二条天皇陵

NTT

Kitano
北野

Dōhoto Art Musm
堂本美術館

Komatsubara
小松原

Kitano-hakubaichō
きたのはくばいちょう

Taishōgun
大将軍

Pref. Med. Coll.
大府立医大(分)

MARUTAMACHI DORI

Kinugasa-Yama
衣笠山

Emperor Ichijō & Horikawa
一条・堀河天皇陵

Ritsumeikan Univ.
立命館大学

Tōji-in
等持院

Rakusei H. Sch.
洛星高校

Tōji-in
等持院

Kyoto Comm. H. Sch.
京都商業高

Yamashiro H. Sch.
山城高校

Hanazono H. Sch.
花園高校

Hanazono Univ.
花園大学

2

Ryōan-ji
竜安寺

Emperor Gosuzaku, Goreizei &
Gosanjō Mausoleum
後朱雀・後冷泉・後三条天皇陵

Ryōanji Garden
竜安寺庭園

Ryōanji
竜安寺

Tenpōrin-ji
等持院

Ryōanjimichi
リょうあんじみち

Taniguchi
谷口

Myōshinji
みょうしんじ

Kelshun-in
桂春院

Myōshin-ji
妙心寺

DaIshin-in
大心院

Taizō-in
退蔵院

Rinkō-in
麟祥院

Hōjō Garden
方丈庭園

Tōrin-in
東林院

Hanazono
花園

3

Emperor Murakami Mausoleum
村上天皇陵

Sch. for the Deaf
聾学校

Ninna-ji
仁和寺

Kondō
金堂

Reihō-kan
霊宝館

Rengei-ji
蓮華寺

Omuro
御室

Omuro
おむろ

Narabiga-Oka
双ヶ岡

Narabigaoka Hosp.
双ヶ岡病院

Hōkongō-in
法金剛院

UKYŌ-KU

4

Emperor En'yū Mausoleum
円融天皇陵

Emperor Kōkō Mausoleum
光孝天皇陵

KEIFUKU 京福 KITANO LINE 北野線

116

102

Hōun-in
法雲院

Utano
宇多野

Takaoguchi
たかおぐち

Omuro-gawa
御室川

Tokiwa
常盤

5

Nat'l Utano Hosp.
国立宇多病院

ROUTE NO.162
国道162号

SHUZAN-KAIDO 周山街道

Ryōtoku-ji
了徳寺

(Daikondaki-dera)
大根焚寺

Narutaki
鳴滝

Narutaki
鳴滝

Emperor Montoku Mausoleum
文徳天皇陵

Narutaki
なるたき

Tokiwa
ときわ

Sagano H. Sch.
嵯峨野高校

SHIN-MARUTAMACHI DORI 新丸太町通

SAN-IN MAIN LINE 山陰本線

6

Okadono-gawa 音戸川

To Shūzan
至周山

Utano Youth Hostel
宇多野ユースホステル

Montoku-ike
文徳池

SHIN-MARUTAMACHI DORI
新丸太町通

To Saga
至嵯峨

7

Central Kyōto (6)
京都市中心部(6)

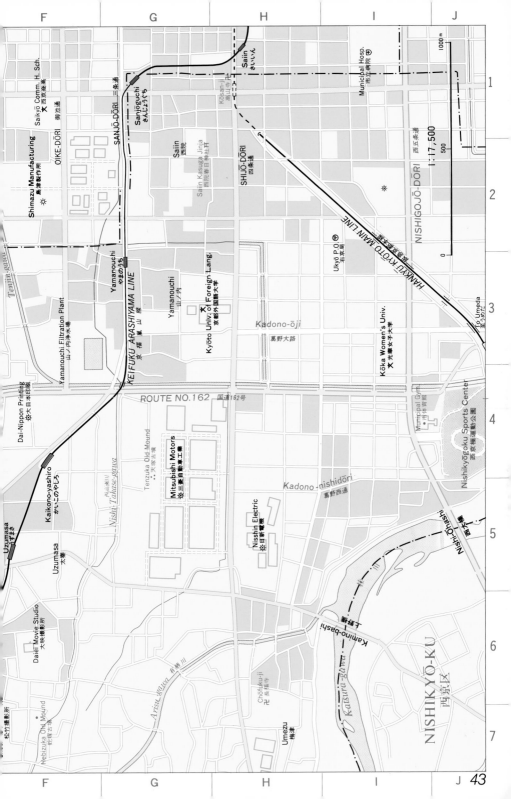

1000 m

Saiin さいいん

Municipal Hosp. 市立病院 ⊞

OIKE-DŌRI 御池通

Shimazu Manufacturing 島津製作所 ✳ 西京衛作所

SANJŌ-DŌRI 三条通 ✳ 西京衛通

Sanjōguchi さんじょうぐち

Saiin 西院

Kōban-ji 高山寺

NISHIGOJŌ-DŌRI 西五条通

1:17,500

500

Saiin Kasuga Jinja 西院春日神社⛩

SHIJŌ-DŌRI 四条通

0

Tenjin-gawa 天神川

Yamanouchi Filtration Plant 山ノ内浄水場

Yamanouchi やまのうち

Yamanouchi 山ノ内

KEIFUKU ARASHIYAMA LINE 京福 嵐山線

Kyōto Univ. of Foreign Lang. 京都外国語大学 ✳

Kadono-ōji 葛野大路

HANKYŪ KYŌTO MAIN LINE 阪急京都本線

Ukyō P.O. ⓟ 右京局

Kōka Women's Univ. 光華女子大学 ✳

To Umeda 梅田へ

Dai-Nippon Printing ✳大日本印刷

Kaikono-yashiro かいこのやしろ

Nishi Takase-gawa 西高瀬川

Tenzuka Old Mound ✳✳天塚古墳

Mitsubishi Motors ✳三菱自動車工業

Kadono-nishidōri 葛野西通

ROUTE NO.162 国道162号

Municipal Gym. 市体育館 ✳

Nishikyōgoku Sports Center 西京極運動公園

Uzumasa うずまさ

Uzumasa 太秦

Nisshin Electric ✳日新電機

Nishi-Ōhashi 西大橋

西京橋

Daiei Movie Studio 大映撮影所

Arisu-gawa 有栖川

Chōfuku-ji 長福寺 卍

Kamino-bashi 上橋

Katsura-gawa 桂川

NISHIKYŌ-KU 西京区

松竹撮影所

Hebizuka Old Mound 蛇塚古墳

Umezu 梅津

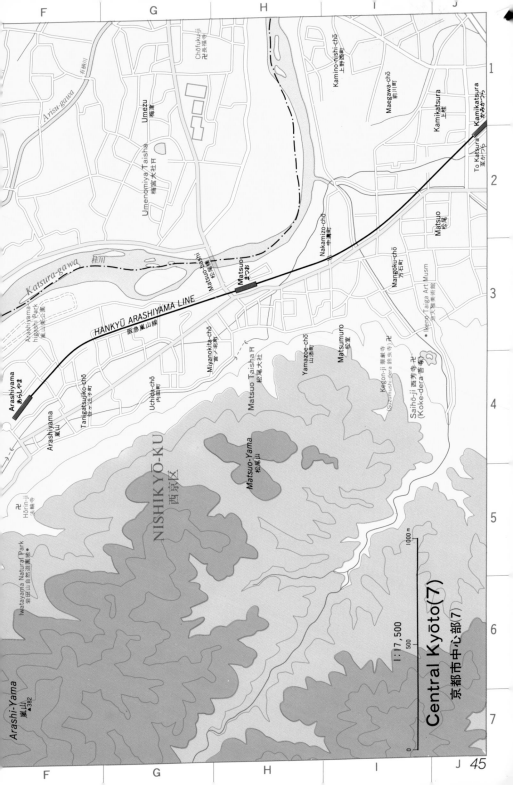

Central Kyōto (7)
京都市中心部(7)

1:17,500

NISHIKYŌ-KU
西京区

HANKYŪ ARASHIYAMA LINE
阪急嵐山線

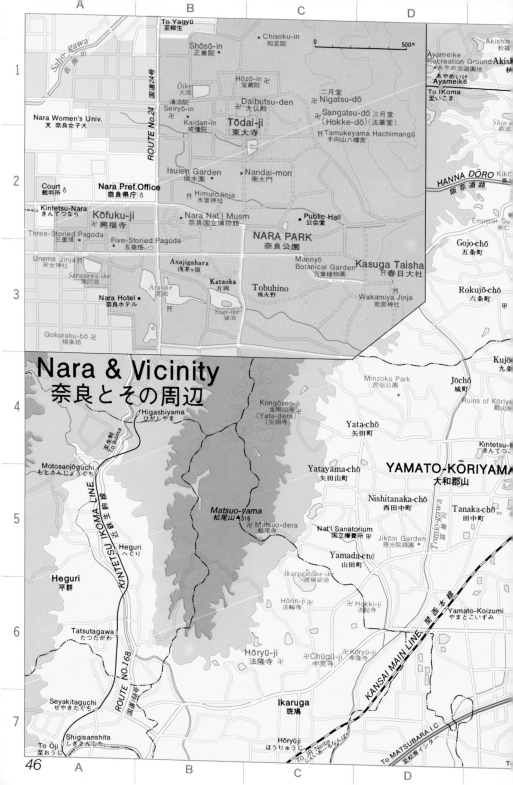

Nara & Vicinity
奈良とその周辺

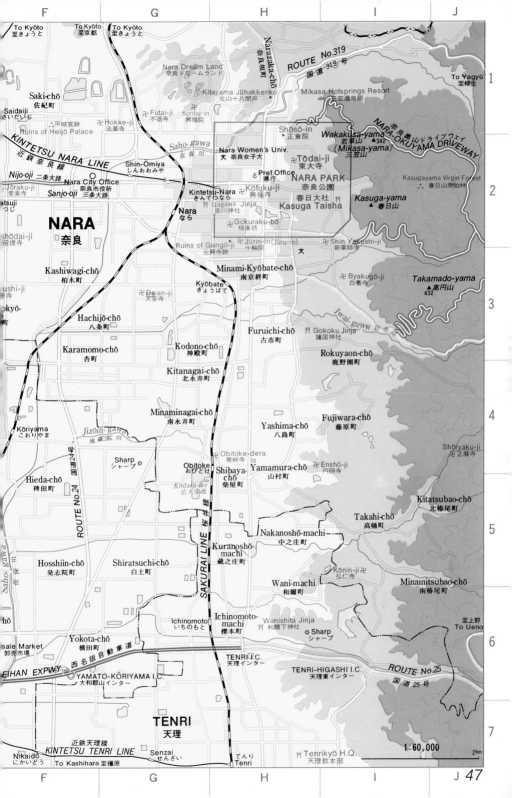

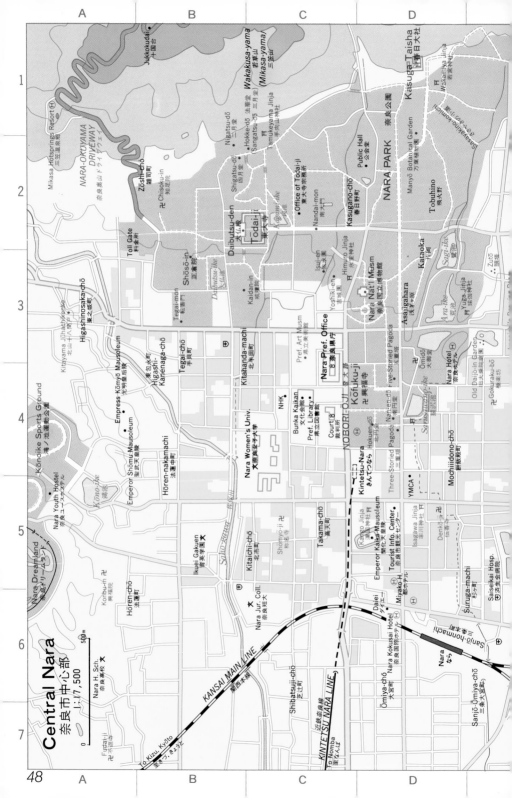

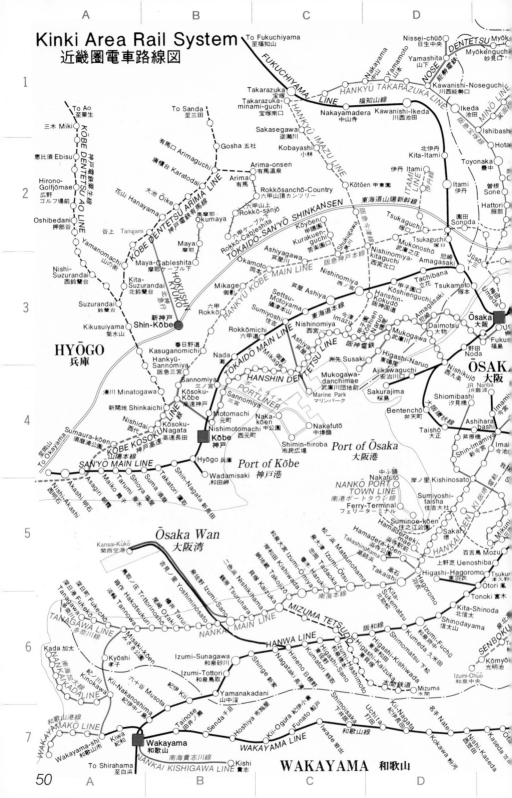

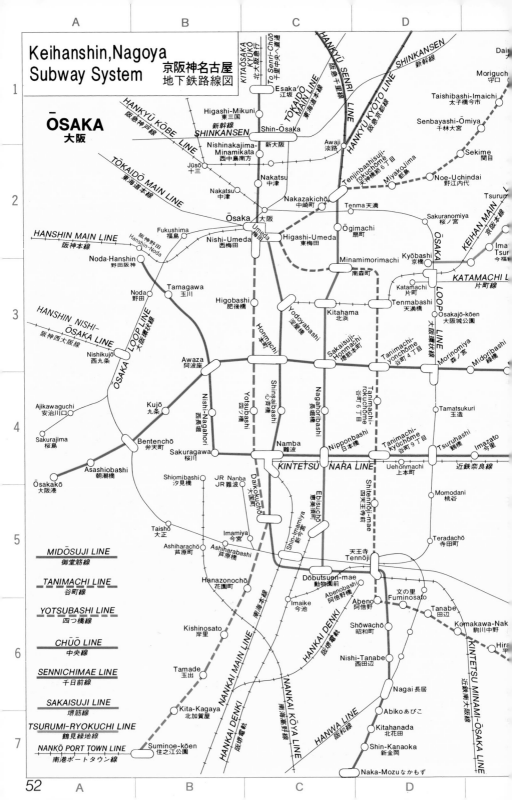

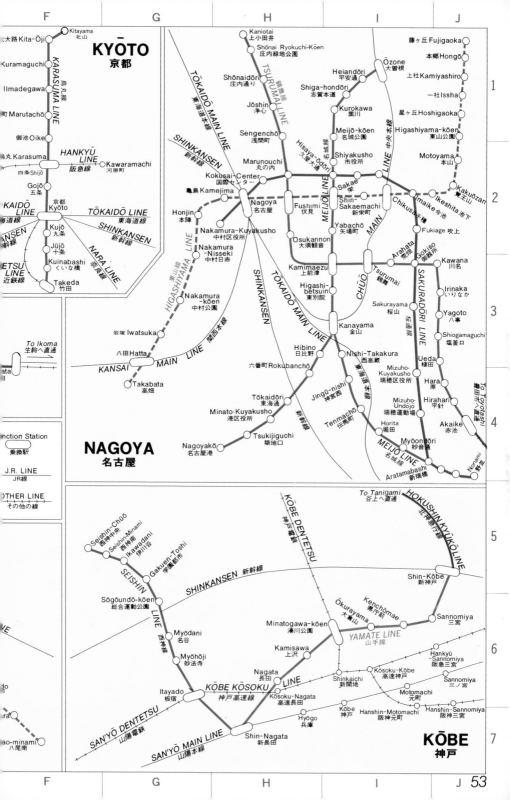

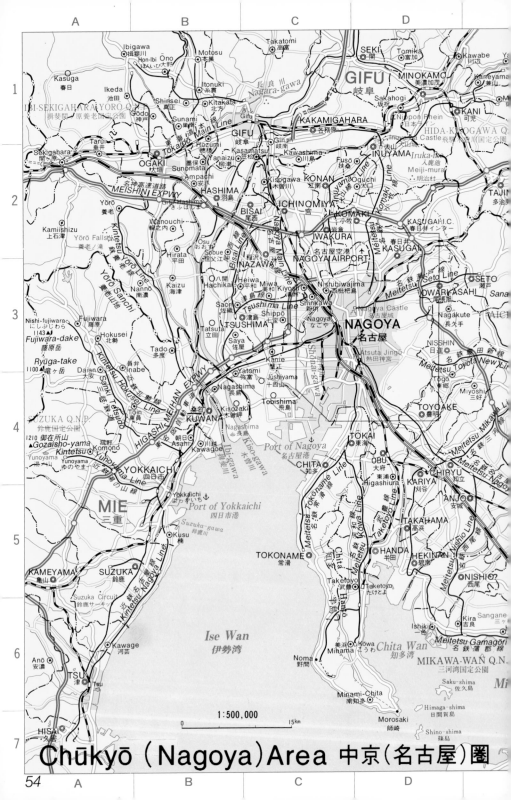

Chūkyō (Nagoya) Area 中京(名古屋)圏

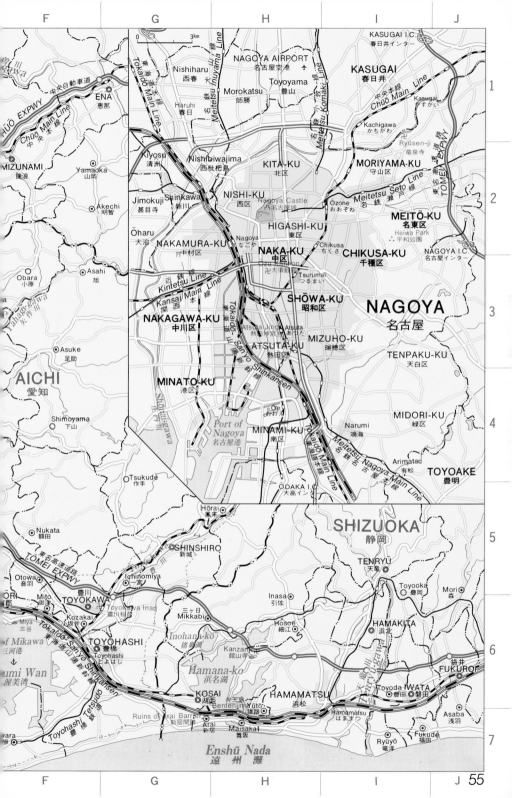

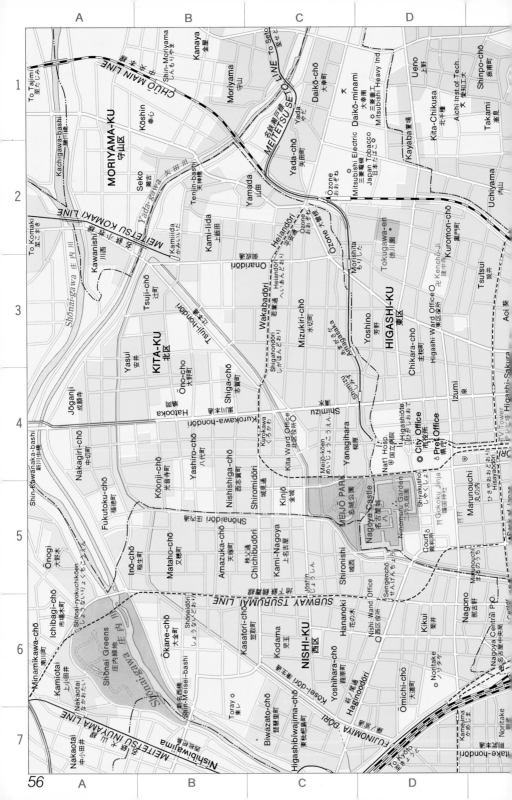

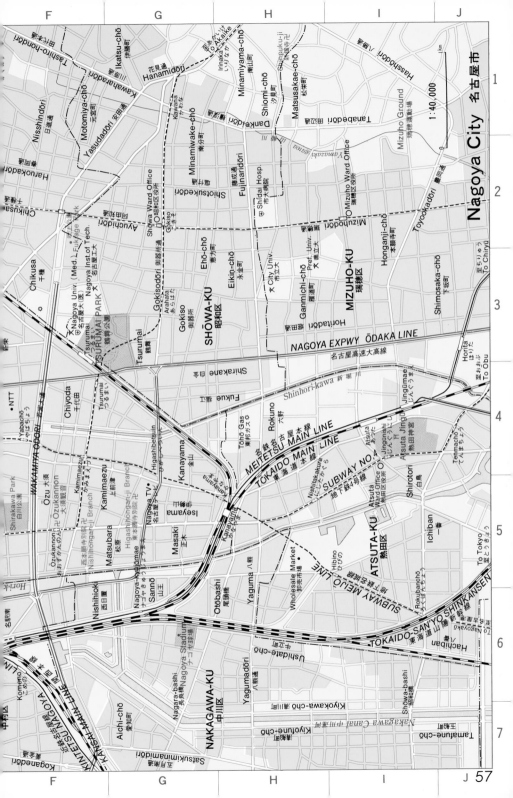

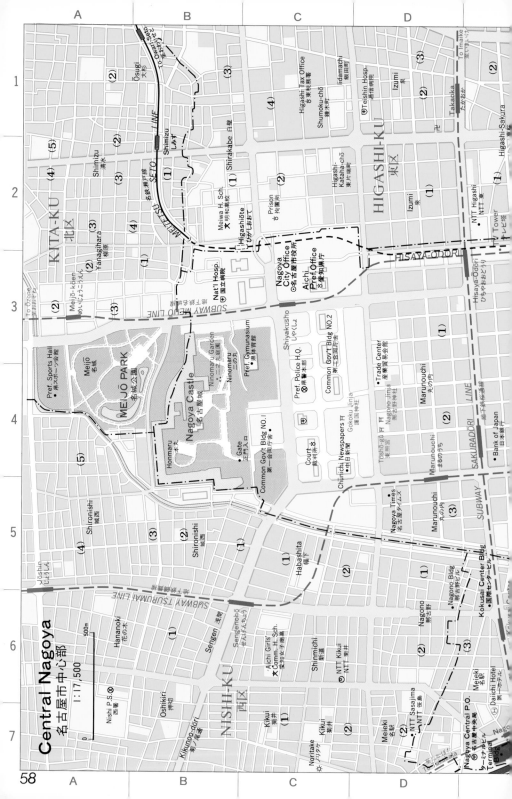

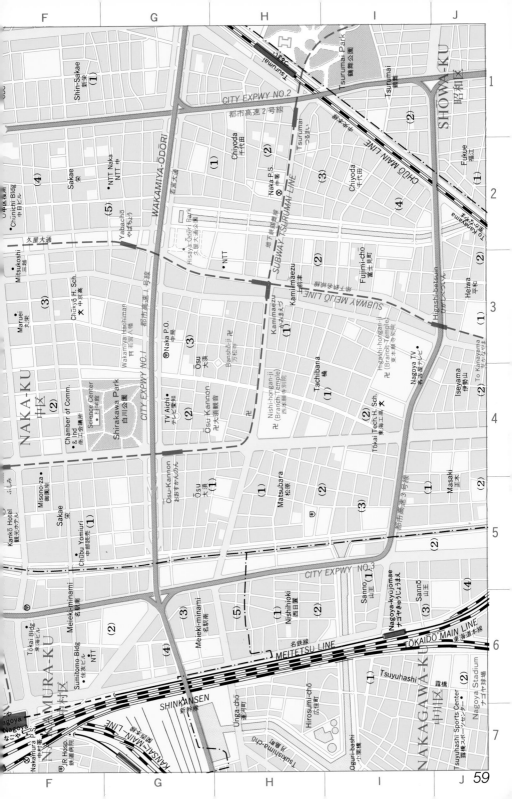

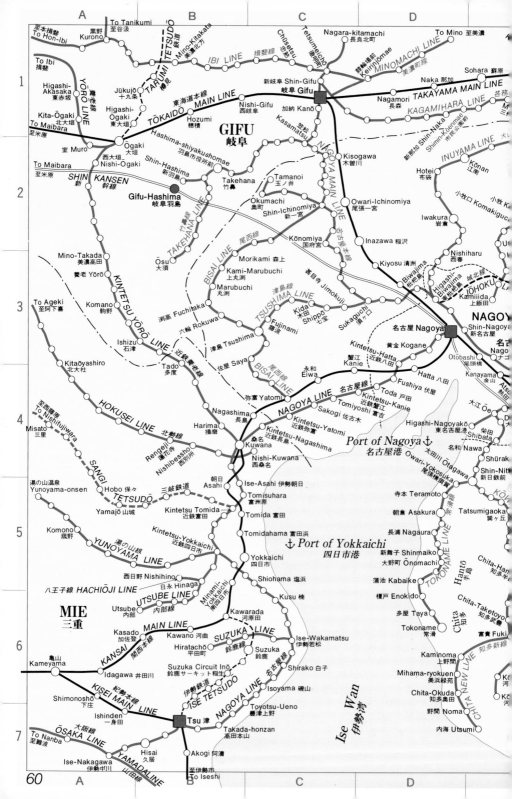

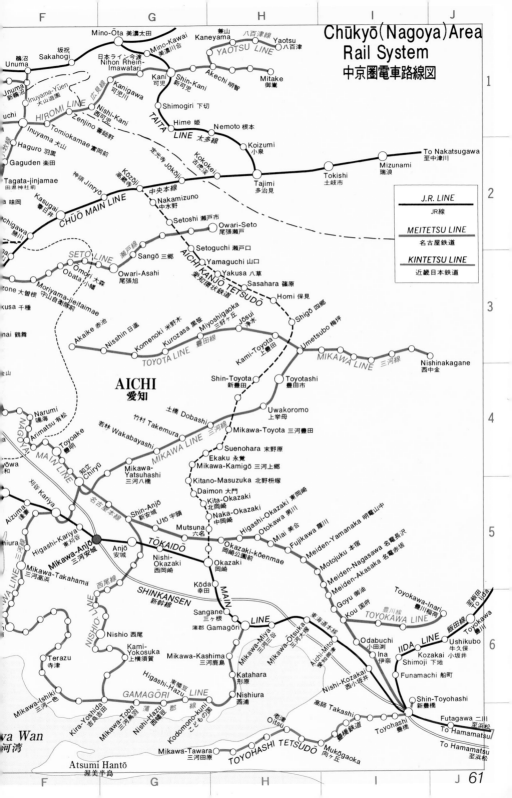

Chūkyō (Nagoya) Area Rail System
中京圏電車路線図

Legend:

J.R. LINE	JR線
MEITETSU LINE	名古屋鉄道
KINTETSU LINE	近畿日本鉄道

Nanki & Ise-Shima
南紀・伊勢志摩

1:700,000

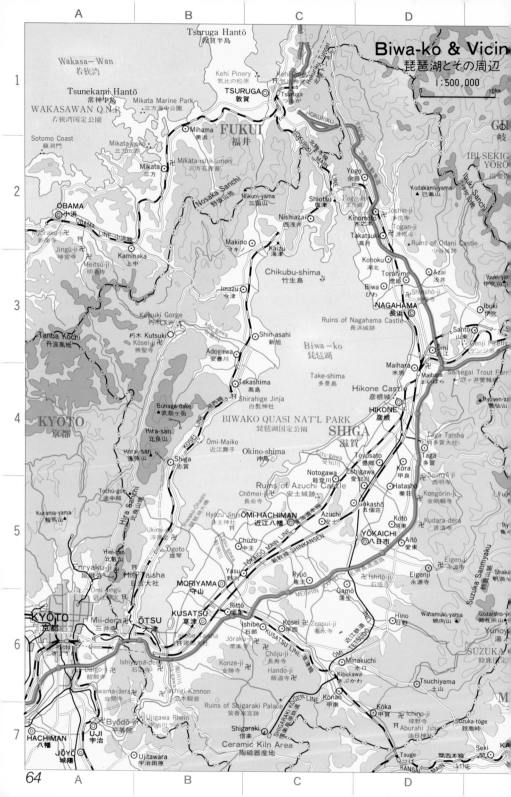

INDEX
索 引（ABC 順）

enobashi Station　阿倍野橋駅 ················ *27* G7
eno-ku　阿倍野区 ································· *7* G5
eno Station　阿倍野駅 ·························· *21* I3
kochō Station　我孫子町駅 ···················· *7* G5
ko Station (Subway)　あびこ駅（地下鉄） ········ *52* D7
urahi jinja　油日神社 ·························· *64* D7
ogawa-chō　安曇川町 ·························· *64* B3
o-chō　阿児町 ································· *63* I2
wan　英虞湾 ································· *63* I2
hi-Kōgen Q.N.P.　愛知高原国定公園 ··········· *54* E3
hi Pref, Office　愛知県庁 ····················· *58* C3
a Station　藍那駅 ····························· *6* A3
i-shi　相生市 ································· *2* A3
o-chō　愛東町 ································· *64* D5
awaguchi Station　安治川口駅 ················· *7* F4
ike Station (Subway)　赤池駅（地下鉄） ·········· *53* J4
shi-nishi I.C.　明石西インター ················· *14* E5
shi Park　明石公園 ··························· *15* F6
shi-shi　明石市 ······························· *15* G6
shi Station　明石駅 ··························· *15* F6
shino-dera　秋篠寺 ··························· *46* E1
agasaka Station　尼ヶ坂駅 ···················· *56* C3
agasaki I.C.　尼崎インター ···················· *7* E2
agasaki-shi　尼崎市 ·························· *6* E3
agasaki Station　尼崎駅 ······················ *7* F3
agatsuji Station　尼ヶ辻駅 ···················· *47* E2
akashini-imasu Jinja　甘樫坐神社 ·············· *49* F4
akashino-oka　甘樫丘 ························· *49* F3
ami Spa　天見温泉 ··························· *9* H4
ami Station　天美駅 ·························· *9* H4
anohashidate　天の橋立 ······················ *3* C1
anokagu-yama　天香久山 ····················· *13* F3
daga-mine　阿彌陀ヶ峰 ······················· *39* G4
da-ji　阿彌陀寺 ······························· *37* H5
no-chō　網野町 ······························· *2* B1
o-chō　安堵町 ······························· *12* D4
o-shi　安城市 ······························· *54* E5
　賀名生 ································· *13* J5
-chō　安濃町 ································· *54* A6
ri-zaki　安乗崎 ······························· *63* I2

Anraku-ji　安楽寺 ····························· *41* I2
An'yō-ji　安養寺 ······························· *38* D4
Aoba-yama　青葉山 ··························· *3* C1
Aogaki-chō　青垣町 ·························· *2* B2
Aoi-bashi (Br)　葵橋 ·························· *37* I5
Aonogahara Station　青野ヶ原駅 ··············· *15* E1
Ao Station　粟生駅 ··························· *14* E2
Aoyama-chō　青山町 ·························· *3* E4
Arahata Station (Subway)　荒畑駅（地下鉄） ······ *57* G3
Arai-chō　新居町 ····························· *55* G7
Aramoto Station　荒本駅 ····················· *51* G3
Arashi-yama　嵐山 ··························· *45* F7
Arashiyama East Park　嵐山東公園 ············· *45* F3
Arashiyama Park　嵐山公園 ··················· *45* E6
Arashiyama Spa　嵐山温泉 ··················· *44* D7
Arashiyama Sta. (Hankyū Line)　嵐山駅（阪急線） ·· *45* F4
Arashiyama Sta. (Keifuku Line)　嵐山駅（京福線） ·· *44* E5
Arida-gawa　有田川 ·························· *62* A3
Arida-shi　有田市 ···························· *62* B3
Arimaguchi Station　有馬口駅 ················· *6* B1
Arima-onsen Station　有馬温泉駅 ·············· *6* C1
Arima Spa　有馬温泉 ························· *6* C1
Arisugawa Station　有栖川駅 ················· *44* E2
Asagiri Station　朝霧駅 ······················ *15* G6
Asago-chō　朝来町 ··························· *2* A2
Asahi-chō　朝日町 ···························· *54* B4
Asahi-ku　旭区 ······························· *20* B1
Asaka Station　浅香駅 ······················· *7* G5
Asakura Station　朝倉駅 ····················· *13* F2
Asama-yama　朝熊山 ························· *63* I1
Asashiobashi Station (Subway)
　朝潮橋駅（地下鉄） ························ *52* A4
Ashiharabashi Stationn　芦原橋駅 ·············· *26* B4
Ashiharachō Station　芦原町駅 ··············· *26* B4
Ashiya-shi　芦屋市 ·························· *6* D3
Ashiya Station　芦屋駅 ······················ *6* D3
Asia & Pacific Trade Center (ATC)
　アジア太平洋トレードセンター ················ *6* E4
Asuka-dera　飛鳥寺（Ago-in 安居院） ··········· *49* F3
Asuka-gawa　飛鳥川 ························· *49* G3

Asuka-mura 明日香村	49	I 4
Asukani-imasu Jinja 飛鳥坐神社	49	F2
Asuka State Park 飛鳥国営公園	49	F4
Asuka Station 飛鳥駅	49	I 7
Asuke-chō 足助町	55	F3
Atago-yama 愛宕山	10	C6
Atsuta Jingū 熱田神宮	55	H3
Atsuta-ku 熱田区	55	H3
Atsuta Station 熱田駅	55	H3
Awaji-chō 淡路町	4	C4
Awaji-shima 淡路島	4	B6
Awashima Jinja 淡島神社	62	A2
Awataguchi 粟田口	38	C4
Awata Jinja 粟田神社	38	C4
Awaza Station (Subway) 阿波座駅(地下鉄)	24	A4
Ayabe-shi 綾部市	3	C2
Ayama-chō 阿山町	3	E3
Ayameike Station 菖蒲池駅	12	B4
Azai-chō 浅井町	64	D3
Azuchi-chō 安土町	64	C5
Bashō-dō 芭蕉堂	38	E5
Bentenchō Station 弁天町駅	21	G7
Bentenjima 弁天島	55	H7
Bisai-shi 尾西市	54	C2
Biwa-chō びわ町	64	D3
Biwa-Ko 琵琶湖	64	C3
Biwako-ōhashi 琵琶湖大橋	10	B2
Biwako Q.N.P. 琵琶湖国定公園	64	C4
Bōeki Center Bldg 商工貿易センタービル	19	F5
Bōeki Center Station 貿易センター駅	19	F4
Bukkō-ji 仏光寺	35	H6
Bunaga-dake 武奈ヶ岳	64	B4
Butta-ji 仏陀寺	37	H5
Byakugō-ji 白毫寺	47	I 3
Byōdō-in 平等院	29	I 3
Chawan-zaka 茶わん坂	39	F5
Chayama Station 茶山駅	41	F4
Chihaya-Akasaka-mura 千早赤坂村	9	H3
Chihayaguchi Station 千早口駅	9	H4
Chikatsuasuka Fudokinooka Park		
近つ飛鳥風土記の丘	9	H2
Chikubu-shima 竹生島	64	C3
Chikurin-ji 竹林寺	34	C2
Chikusa-chō 千種町	2	A2
Chikusa-ku 千種区	55	I 2
Chikusa Station 千種駅	56	E2
Chion-in 知恩院	38	D4
Chion-ji 知恩寺(Hyakumanben 百万遍)	41	H5
Chiryū-shi 知立市	54	D4
Chishaku-in 智積院	39	G6
Chisoku-in 知足院	48	
Chita-shi 知多市	54	
Chōfuku-ji 長福寺	43	
Chōju-ji 長寿寺	64	
Chōkō-dō 長講堂	33	
Chōmei-ji 長命寺	64	
Chōraku-ji 長楽寺	38	
Chūgoku-Ikeda I.C. 中国池田インター	7	
Chūgoku-Toyonaka I.C. 中国豊中インター	7	
Chūgū-ji 中宮寺	46	
CHŪŌ-KU (Kōbe City) 中央区(神戸市)	18	
Chūō-Ku (Ōsaka City) 中央区(大阪市)	20	
Chūshojima Station 中書島駅	29	
Chūzu-chō 中主町	64	
Daian-chō 大安町	54	
Daian-ji 大安寺	47	
Daibutsu-den 大仏殿	48	
Daiei Movie Studio 大映撮影所	43	
Daifugen-dake 大普賢岳	62	
Daifuku Station 大福駅	51	
Daigo-ji 醍醐寺	29	
Daihōon-ji		
大報恩寺(Senbon Shakadō 千本釈迦堂)	36	
Daikaku-ji 大覚寺	44	
Daimotsu Station 大物駅	7	
Dainichi Station (Subway) 大日駅(地下鉄)	52	
Daiō-zaki 大王崎	63	
Daisen-in 大仙院	36	
Daitoku-ji 大徳寺	36	
Daitokuji-hōjō Garden 大徳寺方丈庭園	36	
Daitō-shi 大東市	7	
Daitō-Tsurumi I.C. 大東鶴見インター	7	
Daiun-in 大雲院	38	
Dalkokuchō Station (Subway) 大国町駅(地下鉄)	26	
Dedo Station (Subway) 出戸駅(地下鉄)	53	
Demachi-yanagi Station 出町柳駅	41	
Denkō-ji 伝香寺	48	
Dōbutsuen-mae Station (Subway)		
動物園前駅(地下鉄)	26	
Dōjima 堂島	23	
Dōjō-ji 道成寺	62	
Dōju-in 同聚院	39	
Dōmoto Art Musm 堂本美術館	36	
Dōmyōji Station 道明寺駅	7	
Dorohatchō Gorge 瀞八丁	62	
Dōsen-ji 洞泉寺	47	
Dōshishamae Station 同志社前駅	11	
Dōshisha Univ. 同志社大学	37	
Dōshisha Women's Univ. 同志社女子大学	37	
Ebisuchō Station 恵比須町駅	26	

isu Jinja 恵比須神社	38	E6
higawa-chō 愛知川町	64	D5
eyama Park 会下山公園	16	C4
fuku-ji 叡福寺	9	H2
gen-ji 永源寺	64	D5
genji-chō 永源寺町	64	D5
kan-dō 永観堂(Zenrin-ji 禅林寺)	38	B2
kō-ji 永興寺	38	E1
zan-ji 栄山寺	13	H4
nperor Nintoku Mausolea 仁徳天皇陵	7	G6
a-shi 恵那市	55	G1
jō-ji 円成寺	12	B2
ju Coast 煙樹海岸	62	A4
kō-ji 円光寺	40	D2
mei-ji 延命寺	9	H3
ryaku-ji 延暦寺	28	B1
shō-ji 円照寺	47	I4
toku-in 円徳院	38	E5
aka Station (Subway) 江坂(地下鉄)	52	C1
po Mem.Park 万博記念公園	7	G1
rry-Terminal Station フェリーターミナル駅	50	D5
ower Road フラワーロード	19	F4
shimi-ku 伏見区	29	G3
jigaoka Station (Subway) 藤ヶ丘駅(地下鉄)	53	J1
jiidera I.C. 藤井寺インター	7	H6
jiidera-shi 藤井寺市	7	H5
jiidera Station 藤井寺駅	7	H6
jioka-chō 藤岡町	55	E3
jisaka Station 藤坂駅	11	G5
jita Art Musm 藤田美術館	25	H1
jiwara-chō 藤原町	54	A3
kaebashi Station (Subway) 深江橋駅(地下鉄)	52	E3
kai Station 深井駅	9	F1
kechō Station 深日町駅	50	A6
kekō Station 深日港駅	50	A6
kuchi-in 福智院	48	E3
kuchiyama-shi 福知山市	2	B2
kuroi-shi 袋井市	55	J6
kusaki-chō 福崎町	4	A1
kushima-ku 福島区	20	D6
kushima Station 福島駅	23	I6
minosato Station (Subway) 文の里駅(地下鉄)	21	J2
nado Station 船戸駅	8	C6
naokayama Park 船岡山公園	36	D3
nda-in 芬陀院(Sesshū-ji 雪舟寺)	39	J6
ruichi Station 古市駅	7	H6
se Station 布施駅	7	H4
shimi Inari 伏見稲荷	29	F3
shimi-inari Station 伏見稲荷駅	33	H7
shimi-momoyama Station 伏見桃山駅	29	G4
Fushimi Station 伏見駅	29	G4
Fushimi Station (Subway) 伏見駅(地下鉄)	59	E4
Fushin:an Garden 不審庵庭園	37	F4
Fusō-chō 扶桑町	54	C2
Futai-ji 不退寺	48	A7
Futami-chō 二見町	63	I1
Futamigaura 二見ヶ浦	63	I1
Futatabi-san 再度山	16	E1
Futatsuno Dam 二津野ダム	62	D4
Gakuenmae Station 学園前駅	51	H3
Gakuen-toshi Station (Subway) 学園都市駅(地下鉄)	15	G5
Gamagōri-shi 蒲郡市	55	E6
Gamō-chō 蒲生町	64	C6
Gansen-ji 岩船寺	12	B2
Geinō-chō 芸濃町	3	E3
Gifu-shi 岐阜市	54	C1
Gojō-in 護浄院(Kiyoshi-Kōjin 清荒神)	35	I2
Ginan-chō 岐南町	54	C1
Ginkaku-ji 銀閣寺(Jishō-ji 慈照寺)	41	H2
Giō-ji 祇王寺	44	C7
Gion 祇園	38	D6
Gion Corner ギオンコーナー	38	E6
Gobō-shi 御坊市	62	B4
Gochaku Station 御着駅	14	C3
Gōdo-chō 神戸町	54	B1
Gojō-ōhashi (Br.) 五条大橋	33	H1
Gojō-shi 五条市	13	H5
Gojō Station 五条駅	13	H5
Gojō Station 五条駅	33	H1
Gojō Station (Subway) 五条駅(地下鉄)	33	G1
Gojō Tenjinsha 五条天神社	33	F1
Gojō-zaka 五条坂	39	F5
Gokasho Wan 五ヶ所湾	63	H2
Gokiso Station (Subway) 御器所駅(地下鉄)	57	G2
Gokurakubashi Station 極楽橋駅	9	G7
Gokuraku-bō 極楽坊	48	E4
Gomadan-zan 護摩壇山	62	C3
Gongen Dam 権現ダム	14	E3
Goō Jinja 護王神社	35	G1
Goryō (Kamigoryō) Jinja 御霊(上御霊)神社	37	G4
Gose-shi 御所市	13	G4
Gose Station 御所駅	13	F4
Goshiki-chō 五色町	4	A5
Goshiki-zuka 五色塚	15	G6
Gufuku-ji 弘福寺	49	H3
Habikino-shi 羽曳野市	9	H1
Haga-chō 波賀町	2	A2
Haginochaya Station 萩ノ茶屋駅	26	D7
Hagoromo Station 羽衣駅	7	F6

Haibara-chō 榛原町	5	J5	Hibino Station (Subway) 日比野駅（地下鉄）	57	I
Haibara Station 榛原駅	13	E1	Hidaka-chō 日高町	62	B
Hajinosato Station 土師ノ里駅	51	F5	Hidaka-chō 日高町	2	A
Hakken-zan 八剣山	62	E3	Hidaka-gawa 日高川	62	B
Hakotsukuri Station 箱作駅	8	B5	Hida-Kisogawa Q.N.P. 飛騨木曽川国定公園	54	D
Hakusan-chō 白山町	3	E4	Hiei-zan 比叡山	28	B
Hamadera Station 浜寺駅	9	F1	Higashi-betsuin Station (Subway)		
Hamajima-chō 浜島町	63	I 2	東別院駅（地下鉄）	59	I
Hamakita-shi 浜北市	55	I 6	Higashi-Hanazono Station 東花園駅	51	G
Hamamatsu-shi 浜松市	55	H6	Higashi-hongan-ji 東本願寺	33	F
Hamana Ko 浜名湖	55	G6	Higashi-Ikoma Station 東生駒駅	51	H
Hamaōtsu Station 浜大津駅	28	E1	Higashi-Kaizuka Station 東貝塚駅	8	D
Hamasaka-chō 浜坂町	2	A1	Higashi-Kakogawa Station 東加古川駅	14	E
Hanakuma Station (Subway) 花隈駅（地下鉄）	18	C5	Higashi-Kishiwada Station 東岸和田駅	8	E
Hanano-tera 花の寺	10	E6	Higashi-ku (Nagoya City) 東区（名古屋市）	58	D
Hanase-tōge 花背峠	10	A4	Higashi-Mikuni Sta. (Subway) 東三国駅（地下鉄）	52	C
Hanaten Station 放出駅	7	H4	Higashi-Nada-ku 東灘区	6	C
Hanazono 花園	42	D3	Higashinari-ku 東成区	7	G
Hanazonochō Sta. (Subway) 花園町駅（地下鉄）	52	B5	Higashi-Neyagawa Station 東寝屋川駅	7	I
Hanazono-mura 花園村	62	C3	Higashiōsaka-kita I.C. 東大阪北インター	7	H
Hanazono Station 花園駅	42	E3	Higashiōsaka-minami I.C. 東大阪南インター	7	H
Hanazono Univ. 花園大学	42	E2	Higashi-Ōsaka-shi 東大阪市	7	H
Handa-shi 半田市	54	D5	Higashiōtani 東大谷	38	D
Handō-ji 飯道寺	64	C6	Higashiōte Station 東大手駅	58	B
Hankyū Sannomiya Sta. 阪急三宮駅	18	E4	Higashi-Sano Station 東佐野駅	8	D
Hankyū-Umeda Station 阪急梅田駅	23	G4	Higashi-Suma Station 東須磨駅	16	A
Hannan I.C. 阪南インター	8	C5	Higashi-Sumiyoshi-ku 東住吉区	7	G
Hannan-shi 阪南市	8	B5	Higashi-Umeda Station (Subway)		
Hanshin-Noda Station 阪神野田駅	20	D6	東梅田駅（地下鉄）	23	H
Hanshin-Umeda Station 阪神梅田駅	23	H5	Higashiura-chō 東浦町	54	D
Hara Station (Subway) 原駅（地下鉄）	53	J4	Higashiura-chō 東浦町	4	C
Harborland ハーバーランド	18	C7	Higashiyama-bashi (Br.) 東山橋	33	H
Harima-chō 播磨町	14	D5	Higashiyama Driveway 東山ドライブウェイ	39	F
Haruki Station 春木駅	8	E2	Higashiyama-kōen Sta. (Subway)		
Hase-dera 長谷寺	13	E2	東山公園駅（地下鉄）	53	J
Hasedera Station 長谷寺駅	13	E2	Higashiyama-ku 東山区	38	E
Hashima-shi 羽島市	54	B2	Higashiyama-sanjō Sta. 東山三条駅	38	C
Hashimoto-shi 橋本市	9	H5	Higashiyama Tunnel 東山トンネル	39	H
Hashimoto Station 橋本駅	9	H5	Higashi-yodogawa-ku 東淀川区	22	A
Hatakeda Station 畠田駅	12	D5	Higashiyoshino-mura 東吉野村	13	H
Hatashō-chō 秦荘町	64	D5	Higobashi Station (Subway) 肥後橋駅（地下鉄）	24	C
Hatta Station (Subway) 八田駅（地下鉄）	53	G3	Hikami-chō 氷上町	2	B
Hattorigawa Station 服部川駅	51	G4	Hikigawa-chō 日置川町	62	C
Hayama Kannon 葉山観音	40	D2	Hikone Castle 彦根城	64	D
Hazu-chō 幡豆町	54	E6	Hikone-shi 彦根市	64	D
Heguri-chō 平群町	12	C5	Himeji Castle 姫路城	14	E
Heian-dōri Station (Subway) 平安通駅（地下鉄）	56	C3	Himeji I.C. 姫路インター	14	C
Heian Jingū 平安神宮	38	B4	Himejima Station 姫島駅	20	C
Heiwa-chō 平和町	54	C3	Himeji-shi 姫路市	14	E
Heiwa Park 平和公園	55	I 2	Himeji Station 姫路駅	14	E
Hekinan-shi 碧南市	54	D5	Himuro Jinja 氷室神社	48	C
Henshō-ji 遍照寺	44	C3	Hineno Station 日根野駅	8	D

Hino-chō　日野町　…………… 64　D6
Hino-misaki　日ノ御埼　………… 62　A4
Hinooka Station　日ノ岡駅　……… 39　F1
Hioka Station　日岡駅　………… 14　D4
Hirahari Station (Subway)　平針駅(地下鉄)　……… 53　J4
Hirahata Station　平端駅　……… 46　E7
Hirakata-shi　枚方市　………… 7　I1
Hirakatashi Station　枚方市駅　……… 11　G6
Hirano Jinja　平野神社　……… 36　B5
Hirano-ku　平野区　…………… 7　H5
Hirano Station　平野駅　……… 7　G5
Hirano Station (Subway)　平野駅(地下鉄)　……… 52　E6
Hirano View Park　平野展望公園　…… 16　D3
Hiraoka Station　枚岡駅　……… 51　G3
Hira-san　比良山　……………… 64　B4
Hirokawa-chō　広川町　………… 62　B4
Hirosawano-ike　広沢池　……… 44　B3
Hisai-shi　久居市　……………… 54　A7
Hisaya-ōdōri Station (Subway)
　久屋大通駅(地下鉄)　…………… 58　D3
Hiyodorigoe Forest Park　ひよどりごえ森林公園　‥ 16　A3
Hiyodorigoe Station　鵯越駅　……… 16　B3
Hiyodori View Park　ひよどり展望公園　………… 16　C4
Hiyoshi-chō　日吉町　…………… 3　C2
Hōden Station　宝殿駅　………… 14　D3
Hōkan-ji　法観寺(Yasaka Tower 八坂の塔)　…… 38　E5
Hokke-dō　法華堂(Sangatsu-dō 三月堂)　…… 48　B2
Hokke-ji　法華寺　……………… 47　G1
Hokki-ji　法起寺　……………… 46　D6
Hōkō-ji　方広寺　……………… 39　G6
Hōkoku-Byō　豊国廟　…………… 39　G4
Hōkongō-in　法金剛院　………… 42　D4
Hokudan-chō　北淡町　………… 4　B5
Hokusei-chō　北勢町　………… 54　A3
Hōkyō-in　宝筐院　……………… 44　C5
Hōkyō-ji　宝鏡寺(Ningyō-dera 人形寺)　…… 37　F4
Hōnen-in　法然院　……………… 41　I2
Hongō Station (Subway)　本郷駅(地下鉄)　…… 53　J1
Hongū-chō　本宮町　…………… 62　D5
Honjin Station (Subway)　本陣駅(地下鉄)　…… 53　G2
Honmachi Station (Subway)　本町駅(地下鉄)　…… 24　D4
Honnō-ji　本能寺　……………… 35　I4
Honpō-ji　本法寺　……………… 37　F4
Honryū-ji　本隆寺　……………… 36　E5
Hōraikyō　蓬莱峡　……………… 6　D1
Hōrai-san　蓬莱山　……………… 64　B4
Hōrin-ji　法輪寺(Daruma-dera だるま寺)　…… 34　C2
Hōrin-ji　法輪寺　……………… 15　G3
Hōrin-ji　法輪寺　……………… 45　F5
Hōrin-ji　法輪寺　……………… 46　C6
Horita Station　堀田駅　………… 57　J3
Hōryū-ji　法隆寺　……………… 46　C6

Hōryūji I.C.　法隆寺インター　………… 12　D4
Hōryūji Station　法隆寺駅　……… 46　C7
Hoshida Station　星田駅　……… 7　I2
Hoshigaoka Station (Subway)　星ヶ丘駅(地下鉄)　… 53　J1
Hoshiya Station　布施屋駅　……… 8　C7
Hōsono Station　祝園駅　……… 11　H4
Hōun-in　法雲院　……………… 42　E5
Hōzen-ji　法善寺　……………… 26　E2
Hōzenji Station　法善寺駅　……… 51　G5
Hozu-gawa　保津川　…………… 44　E6
Hozu-kyō　保津峡　……………… 44　D7
Hozumi-chō　穂積町　…………… 54　B1
Hyōgo-ku (Kōbe City)　兵庫区(神戸市)　…… 18　A3
Hyōgo Station　兵庫駅　………… 16　D5
Hyōtan-yama Station　瓢箪山駅　…… 51　G3
Hyōzu Junja　兵主神社　………… 64　B5

Ibaraki I.C.　茨木インター　………… 7　H1
Ibaraki-shi　茨木市　…………… 7　H1
Ibaraki Station　茨木駅　………… 7　H1
Ibi-gawa　揖斐川　……………… 54　B4
Ibigawa-chō　揖斐川町　………… 54　B1
Ibi-Sekigahara-Yōrō Q.N.P.
　揖斐関ヶ原養老国定公園　……… 3　E1
Ibogawa-chō　揖保川町　………… 2　A3
Ibuki-chō　伊吹町　……………… 64　E3
Ibuki-yama　伊吹山　…………… 64　E3
Ichiba Station　市場駅　………… 15　E3
Ichijima-chō　市島町　…………… 2　B2
Ichijō-ji　一乗寺　……………… 14　D2
Ichijōji Station　一乗寺駅　……… 40　E4
Ichikawa-chō　市川町　………… 4　A1
Ichino-ji　櫟野寺　……………… 2　A2
Ichinomiya-chō　一宮町　………… 4　B5
Ichinomiya-chō　一宮町　………… 54　C2
Ichinomiya-shi　一宮市　………… 47　G6
Ichinomoto Station　櫟本駅　……… 3　E4
Ichishi-chō　一志町　…………… 11　G4
Ide-chō　井出町　……………… 2　A4
Ieshima-chō　家島町　…………… 3　E3
Iga-chō　伊賀町　……………… 63　G1
Iinan-chō　飯南町　……………… 63　G1
Iitaka-chō　飯高町　……………… 18　D3
Ijinkan-dōri　異人館通り　………… 46　C7
Ikaruga-chō　班鳩町　…………… 15　G5
Ikawadani Jct.　伊川谷ジャンクション　…… 53　G5
Ikawadani Station (Subway)　伊川谷駅(地下鉄)　… 54　A1
Ikeda-chō　池田町　……………… 7　F1
Ikeda-shi　池田市　……………… 7　F1
Ikeda Station　池田駅　………… 62　E3
Ikehara Dam　池原ダム　………… 62　E3

Ikeshita Station (Subway)　池下駅（地下鉄）········· 57　E1
Ikoma-shi　生駒市 ································· 12　B5
Ikoma Station　生駒駅 ····························· 12　B5
Ikoma-yama　生駒山 ······························· 12　C5
Ikukunitama Jinja　生国魂神社 ················ 27　G3
Ikuno-chō　生野町 ································· 2　B2
Ikuno-ku　生野区 ·································· 27　I6
Ikuta Jinja　生田神社 ···························· 18　E3
Imadegawa Station (Subway)　今出川駅（地下鉄）·· 37　G5
Imai　今井 ·· 13　F3
Imaike Station　今池駅 ···························· 26　D7
Imaike Station (Subway)　今池駅（地下鉄）·········· 56　E2
Imakumano Jinja　新熊野神社 ·················· 39　H6
Imakumano Kannon-ji　今熊野観音寺 ········· 39　I5
Imamiya Ebisu Jinja　今宮戎神社 ············· 26　E5
Imamiya-ebisu Station　今宮戎駅 ············· 26　E5
Imamiya Jinja　今宮神社 ························· 36　D2
Imamiya Station　今宮駅 ························· 26　C5
Imasato Station (Subway)　今里駅（地下鉄）········ 21　G1
Imazu-chō　今津町 ································· 64　B3
Imazu Station　今津駅 ···························· 6　D3
Inabe-chō　員弁町 ································· 54　A4
Inagawa-chō　猪名川町 ···························· 4　E2
Inami-chō　稲美町 ································· 15　E4
Inami-chō　印南町 ································· 62　B5
Inari Station　稲荷駅 ···························· 29　F4
Inazawa-shi　稲沢市 ······························ 54　C3
Industrial Arts & Textile Univ.　工芸繊維大学 ··· 40　C5
Ine-chō　伊根町 ··································· 3　B1
Injō-ji　引接寺（Senbon Enmadō 千本えんま堂）····· 36　D4
Inunaki-yama　犬鳴山 ···························· 8　E5
Inuyama Castle　犬山城 ···························· 54　D1
Inuyama-shi　犬山市 ······························ 54　D2
Irinaka Station (Subway)　いりなか駅（地下鉄）····· 57　H1
Isagawa Jinja　率川神社 ························· 48　D5
Ise Jingō　伊勢神宮 ······························ 63　H1
Ise-shi　伊勢市 ··································· 63　H1
Ise-Shima N.P.　伊勢志摩国立公園 ············ 63　H1
Ishibashi Station　石橋駅 ······················· 7　F1
Ishibe-chō　石部町 ································· 64　C6
Ishibutai Old Mound　石舞台古墳 ············· 49　I2
Ishiki-chō　一色町 ································· 54　D6
Ishikiri Station　石切駅 ························· 7　I4
Ishitō-ji　石塔寺 ································· 64　D5
Ishiyama-dera　石山寺 ···························· 10　E2
Isobe-chō　磯部町 ································· 63　I2
Isonokami Jingū　石上神宮 ······················ 12　D2
Issha Station (Subway)　一社駅（地下鉄）·········· 53　J1
Isui-en　依水園 ··································· 48　C3
Itami-shi　伊丹市 ································· 7　E2
Itami Station　伊丹駅 ···························· 7　F2
Itayado Station　板宿駅 ························· 16　A6

Iwade-chō　岩出町 ································· 62　E
Iwade Station　岩出駅 ···························· 8　C
Iwaki-yama　岩湧山 ······························· 9　G
Iwakura-shi　岩倉市 ······························ 54　C
Iwakura Station　岩倉駅 ·························· 28　C
Iwami Station　石見駅 ···························· 12　E
Iwashimizu Hachimangū　石清水八幡宮 ········ 29　J
Iwataki-chō　岩滝町 ······························ 3　E
Iwata-shi　盤田市 ································· 55　I
Iwatayama Natural Park　岩田山自然遊園地 ··· 45　F
Iwatsuka Station (Subway)　岩塚駅（地下鉄）······ 53　G
Iwaya Station　岩屋駅 ···························· 19　J
Izimisano-shi　泉佐野市 ························· 8　C
Izumi-Fuchū Station　和泉府中駅 ············· 9　E
Izumigaoka Station　泉ヶ丘駅 ··················· 9　F
Izumi-Hashimoto Station　和泉橋本駅 ········ 8　D
Izumi-Ōtsu-shi　泉大津市 ······················· 8　E
Izumiōtsu Station　泉大津駅 ···················· 8　E
Izumisano Station　泉佐野駅 ···················· 8　D
Izumi-shi　和泉市 ································· 9　E
Izumi-Sunagawa Station　和泉砂川駅 ········· 8　C
Izumi-Tottori Station　和泉鳥取駅 ············ 8　C
Izushi-chō　出石町 ································· 2　E

JR Nanba Station　JR難波駅 ···················· 26　D
Jakkō-in　寂光院 ································· 28　A
Jikishi-an　直指庵 ································· 44　A
Jikōin Garden　慈光院庭園 ······················ 46　D
Jingo-ji　神護寺 ································· 28　C
Jingūmae Station　神宮前駅 ···················· 57　I
Jingūnishi Station (Subway)　神宮西駅（地下鉄）··· 57　I
Jishin-in　慈心院 ································· 39　F
Jishō-ji　慈照寺（Ginkaku-ji 銀閣寺）··········· 41　H
Jissō-ji　実相寺 ································· 28　E
Jizō-in　地蔵院（Tsubaki-dera 椿寺）············ 36　F
Jōdoji　浄土寺 ··································· 41　I
Jōdo-ji　浄土寺 ··································· 15　F
Jōhoku Park　城北公園 ···························· 20　A
Jōhon-rendai-ji　上品蓮台寺 ···················· 36　C
Jōjakkō-ji　常寂光寺 ···························· 44　C
Jōju-in Garden　成就院庭園 ···················· 39　F
Jōnan-gū　城南宮 ································· 29　G
Jōraku-ji　常楽寺 ································· 47　F
Jōraku-ji　常楽寺 ································· 64　C
Jōruri-ji　浄瑠璃寺 ······························ 12　E
Jōshin-ji　浄信寺 ································· 64　D
Jōtenkaku Art Musm　承天閣美術館 ············ 37　H
Jōtō-ku　城東区 ································· 7　H
Jōyō I.C.　城陽インター ························· 11　G
Jōyō-shi　城陽市 ································· 11　G
Jōzen-ji　上善寺 ································· 37　H
Jūbu-san　鷲峰山 ································· 11　G
Jūjō Station (Subway)　十条駅（地下鉄）·········· 33　F

ru-in 十輪院	48	E3	
sō-ōhashi (Br.) 十三大橋	23	F7	
sō Station 十三駅	22	D7	
buto-yama 甲山	6	D2	
da 加太	4	C6	
domachi Station 門真市駅	7	H2	
doma I.C. 門真インター	7	H3	
doma-shi 門真市	7	H3	
guyama Station 香久山駅	13	F3	
hada-kyō 香肌峡	62	F1	
ibara-chō 柏原町	2	B2	
idan-in 戒壇院	48	C3	
ijūsen-ji 海住山寺	11	H3	
ikono-yashiro 蚕の社	43	E4	
ikono-yashiro Station 蚕の社駅	43	F4	
inan-shi 海南市	62	B3	
iyū-kan (Ōsaka Aquarium) 海遊館	7	F4	
izuka I.C. 貝塚インター	8	E4	
izuka-shi 貝塚市	8	D3	
izuka Station 貝塚駅	8	D3	
kamigahara-shi 各務原市	54	C1	
kogawa-shi 加古川市	14	D4	
kogawa Station 加古川駅	14	D4	
kuōzan Station (Subway) 覚王山駅（地下鉄）	57	F1	
kurin-ji 鶴林寺	14	D4	
lzu-chō 海津町	54	B3	
mejima Station (Subway) 亀島駅（地下鉄）	53	H2	
meoka-shi 亀岡市	10	C7	
meyama Park 亀山公園	44	E6	
meyama-shi 亀山市	54	A5	
migyō-ku 上京区	36	D6	
miiida Station 上飯田駅	56	B2	
mi-Kitayama-mura 上北山村	63	E3	
mikoma Station 上狛駅	11	I3	
mimaezu Station (Subway) 上前津駅（地下鉄）	59	H3	
minaka-chō 上中町	64	A2	
mino-taishi Station 上ノ太子駅	7	I6	
misawa Station (Subway) 上沢駅（地下鉄）	16	C5	
mi-shima 神島	63	J1	
mi Station 加美駅	7	H5	
mi-Tanabe Station 上田辺駅	11	H4	
mitonda-chō 上富田町	62	C5	
mmaki-chō 上牧町	12	E4	
mo-chō 加茂町	11	I3	
momioya (Shimogamo) Jinja			
加茂御祖（下鴨）神社	37	I4	
mo-ōhashi (Br.) 加茂大橋	37	I6	
mo Station 加茂駅	11	I3	
nahashi Station 金橋駅	13	F4	
nan-chō 河南町	9	H2	
naya-chō 金屋町	62	B3	

Kanayama Station 金山駅	57	H5	
Kanchi-in 観智院	32	D4	
Kandaijin Jinja 菅大臣神社	35	F6	
Kaneyama-chō 兼山町	54	E1	
Kango Jinja 漢国神社	48	D5	
Kangyō-kan 勧業館	38	B5	
Kanie-chō 蟹江町	54	C3	
Kaniman-ji 蟹満寺	11	H3	
Kani-shi 可児市	54	D1	
Kanjirō Kawai Mem. Hall 河井寛次郎記念館	39	F6	
Kankū-ji 観空寺	44	B5	
Kannon-ji 観音寺	34	D2	
Kansai Int'l Airport 関西国際空港	4	D5	
Kansai Science City 関西文化学術研究都市	11	H5	
Kansai Univ. 関西大学	23	F2	
Kansetsu Hashimoto Mem, Hall			
橋本関雪記念館	41	H3	
Kanshin-ji 勧心寺	9	H3	
Kanshū-ji 勧修寺	29	G2	
Kantei-byō 関帝廟	18	C4	
Kanzaki-chō 神崎町	4	A1	
Kanzanji Spa 館山寺温泉	55	H6	
Karasu-chō 香良洲町	3	F4	
Karasuma Station 烏丸駅	35	G5	
Karekinada Coast 枯木灘海岸	62	D6	
Kariya-shi 刈谷市	54	D4	
Kasagi-chō 笠置町	11	H2	
Kasagi Station 笠置駅	11	H2	
Kasagi-yama 笠置山	11	I1	
Kasahara-chō 笠原町	54	E2	
Kasai-shi 加西市	14	D1	
Kasamatsu-chō 笠松町	54	C2	
Kasanui Station 笠縫駅	12	E3	
Kaseda Station 笠田駅	9	F6	
Kashiba I.C. 香芝インター	7	J6	
Kashiba-shi 香芝市	12	E5	
Kashihara Jingū 橿原神宮	13	F3	
Kashihara Jingū Station 橿原神宮駅	13	F3	
Kashihara-shi 橿原市	13	F4	
Kashiwara I.C. 柏原インター	7	I6	
Kashiwara-shi 柏原市	7	I5	
Kashiwara Station 柏原駅	7	I5	
Kasturagi-san 葛城山	8	E5	
Kasuga-chō 春日町	2	B2	
Kasugai-shi 春日井市	55	I1	
Kasugamichi Station (Hankyū Line)			
春日道駅（阪急線）	19	G2	
Kasugamichi Station (Hanshin Line)			
春日道駅（阪神線）	19	H2	
Kasuga Taisha 春日大社	48	D1	
Kasuga-yama 春日山	47	I2	
Kasumi-chō 香住町	2	A1	

Katabirano-tsuji Sta.　惟子の辻駅 ……………… 43　E7
Katamachi Station　片町駅 ……………… 25　I 1
Katano-shi　交野市 ……………… 7　I 2
Katanoshi Station　交野市駅 ……………… 11　H6
Katashimo Station　堅下駅 ……………… 51　G5
Katsuragi-chō　かつらぎ町 ……………… 9　F5
Katsuragi Jinja　葛木神社 ……………… 9　I 3
Katsuragi-san　葛城山 ……………… 13　G5
Katsura Rikyū　桂離宮 ……………… 29　F5
Katsura Station　桂駅 ……………… 29　F6
Katsuura Spa　勝浦温泉 ……………… 62　E6
Kawabe-chō　川辺町 ……………… 62　B4
Kawachi-Eiwa Station　河内永和駅 ……………… 51　F4
Kawachi-Hanazono Station　河内花園駅 ………… 7　I 4
Kawachi-Iwafune Station　河内磐船駅 ……………… 7　J2
Kawachi-Katakami Station　河上堅上駅 ……………… 7　I 6
Kawachi-Kokubu Station　河内国分駅 ……………… 51　G5
Kawachi-Matsubara Station　河内松原駅 …………… 7　H6
Kawachi-Nagano-shi　河内長野市 ……………… 9　G3
Kawachi-nagano Station　河内長野駅 ……………… 9　G3
Kawachi-Yamamoto Station　河内山本駅 …………… 7　I 5
Kawage-chō　河芸町 ……………… 54　A6
Kawagoe-chō　川越町 ……………… 54　B4
Kawai-chō　河合町 ……………… 12　D4
Kawai Jinja　河合神社 ……………… 37　I 4
Kawakami-mura　川上村 ……………… 63　E2
Kawana Station (Subway)　川名駅(地下鉄) ………… 57　G1
Kawanishi-chō　川西町 ……………… 12　D4
Kawanishi-Ikeda Station　川西池田駅 …………… 7　E1
Kawanishi-shi　川西市 ……………… 7　E1
Kawaramachi Station　河原町駅 ……………… 35　I 5
Kawasaki Steel　川崎製鉄 ……………… 19　H3
Kawayu Spa　川湯温泉 ……………… 62　D5
Kaya-chō　加悦町 ……………… 2　B1
Kazan　花山 ……………… 39　F2
Keage Station　蹴上駅 ……………… 38　C3
Keihoku-chō　京北町 ……………… 3　D2
Keishun-in　桂春院 ……………… 42　C3
Kenchū-ji　建中寺 ……………… 56　D3
Kennin-ji　建仁寺 ……………… 38　E6
Kibi-chō　吉備町 ……………… 62　B3
Kibuneguchi Station　貴船口駅 ……………… 28　A4
Kibune-Jinja　貴船神社 ……………… 28　A4
Kibune-yama　貴船山 ……………… 10　B4
Kihō-chō　紀宝町 ……………… 62　E5
Kii-nagashima-chō　紀伊長島町 ……………… 63　G3
Kii-Nagata Station　紀伊長田駅 ……………… 8　D6
Kii-Ogura Station　紀伊小倉駅 ……………… 8　C7
Kii Station　紀伊駅 ……………… 8　B6
Kii-Yamada Station　紀伊山田駅 ……………… 9　H5

Kikō-ji　喜光寺 ……………… 46
Kikusuiyama Station　菊水山駅 ……………… 16
Kimii-dera　紀三井寺 ……………… 62
Kimi-tōge　紀見峠 ……………… 9
Kimitōge Station　紀見峠駅 ……………… 13
Kinkaku-ji　金閣寺(Rokuon-ji 鹿苑寺) ……………… 36
Kinokawa S.A.　紀ノ川サービスエリア ……………… 8
Kinokawa Station　紀ノ川駅 ……………… 8
Kino-Matsushima　紀ノ松島 ……………… 62
Kinomoto-chō　木之本町 ……………… 64
Kinosaki-chō　城崎町 ……………… 2
Kintai-ji　金胎寺 ……………… 11
Kintetsu-Nara Station　近鉄奈良駅 ……………… 47
Kintetsu-Shimoda Station　近鉄下田駅 ………… 51
Kintetsu-Yao Station　近鉄八尾駅 ……………… 51
Kinugasa　衣笠 ……………… 36
Kinugasa-yama　衣笠山 ……………… 36
Kira-chō　吉良町 ……………… 54
Kire-Uriwari Sta. (Subway)　喜連瓜破駅(地下鉄) … 52
Kisaichi Station　私市駅 ……………… 11
Kisei-chō　紀勢町 ……………… 63
Kishibe Station　岸辺駅 ……………… 7
Kishigawa-chō　貴志川町 ……………… 62
Kishinosato Station (Subway)　岸里駅(地下鉄) … 52
Kishi Station　貴志駅 ……………… 51
Kishiwada-Izumi I.C.　岸和田泉インター ………… 9
Kishiwada-shi　岸和田市 ……………… 8
Kishiwada Station　岸和田駅 ……………… 8
Kiso-gawa　木曽川 ……………… 54
Kisogawa-chō　木曽川町 ……………… 54
Kitagata-chō　北方町 ……………… 54
Kitahama Station　北浜駅 ……………… 24
Kita-Hanada Station (Subway)　北花田駅(地下鉄) 52
Kita-Itami Station　北伊丹駅 ……………… 7
Kita-Kagaya Station (Subway)
　北加賀屋駅(地下鉄) ……………… 52
Kita-ku (Kōbe City)　北区(神戸市) ……………… 16
Kita-ku (Nagoya City)　北区(名古屋市) ……………… 55
Kita-ku (Ōsaka City)　北区(大阪市) ……………… 23
Kita-midō　北御堂 ……………… 24
Kitano-chō (Kōbe City)　北野町(神戸市) ………… 18
Kitano-dōri　北野通り ……………… 18
Kitano-hakubaichō Station　北野白梅町駅 ……… 36
Kitano Tenmangū　北野天満宮 ……………… 36
Kitaōji Station (Subway)　北大路駅(地下鉄) ……… 37
Kita-Saga　北嵯峨 ……………… 44
Kita-Senri Station　北千里駅 ……………… 7
Kita-Shinoda Station　北信太駅 ……………… 7
Kitashirakawa　北白川 ……………… 41
Kita-Suzuradai Station　北鈴蘭台駅 ……………… 6
Kita-Tatsumi Sta. (Subway)　北巽駅(地下鉄) …… 52
Kitauchi Station　北宇智駅 ……………… 13

ayama-gawa　北山川 ················· *62* E4
ayama Jūhachikenko　北山十八間戸 ········· *48* A3
ayama-mura　北山村 ················· *62* E4
ayama Station (Subway)　北山駅(地下鉄) ······ *37* H1
wa-chō　紀和町 ················· *62* E4
wa Station　紀和駅 ················· *8* A7
yomizu-dera　清水寺 ················· *39* F4
yomizu-yama　清水山 ················· *39* F3
yomizu-zaka　清水坂 ················· *39* E5
yoshi Kōjin　清荒神 ················· *6* D1
yosu-chō　清洲町 ················· *54* C3
zetsu-kyō　奇絶狭 ················· *62* C5
zu-chō　木津町 ················· *11* I3
zu-gawa　木津川 ················· *11* F5
zugawa Station　木津川駅 ················· *26* A5
zu Station　木津駅 ················· *11* I3
be Bunka Hall　神戸文化ホール ········· *18* B6
be City Office　神戸市役所 ········· *19* F4
be Customhouse　神戸税関 ········· *19* F5
be Municipal Musm　神戸市立博物館 ········· *18* E5
be-Ōhashi (Br,)　神戸大橋 ········· *19* G7
be Portpier Land　神戸ポートピアランド ······ *17* H5
be-Sanda I.C.　神戸三田インター ········· *15* I2
be-shi　神戸市 ················· *4* D3
be Station　神戸駅 ················· *18* C7
be Steel　神戸製鋼 ················· *19* J2
be Univ. (Med.)　神戸大学(医学部) ········· *18* A6
dai-ji　高台寺 ················· *38* E5
dera-chō　香寺町 ················· *14* B1
-dō　革堂 ················· *35* I3
fuku-ji　興福寺 ················· *48* D4
gen-ji　向原寺 ················· *49* F4
ohata Station　木幡駅 ················· *29* H3
ohoku-chō　湖北町 ················· *64* D3
oka-chō　甲賀町 ················· *64* D7
okawa-chō　粉河町 ················· *8* E6
okawa Station　粉河駅 ················· *8* E6
oka Women's Univ.　光華女子大学 ········· *43* I3
oki-ji　高貴寺 ················· *9* I2
okusai Center Station (Subway)
　国際センター駅(地下鉄) ········· *58* E6
omakawa-Nakano Sta. (Subway)
　駒川中野駅(地下鉄) ········· *52* D6
omaki-shi　小牧市 ················· *54* D2
omono-chō　菰野町 ················· *54* A4
ōmyō-ike　光明池 ················· *9* F3
ōmyōike Station　光明池駅 ················· *29* F2
ōmyō-ji　光明寺 ················· *29* G7
ōnan-chō　甲南町 ················· *64* C6
ōnan-shi　江南市 ················· *54* C2
onbu-in　興福院 ················· *48* A5
onbusen-ji　金峰山寺 ················· *62* E2

Konchi-in　金地院 ················· *38* C3
Konda-chō　今田町 ················· *4* C1
Kongōbu-ji　金剛峯寺 ················· *62* C3
Kongō-ji　金剛寺 ················· *9* G3
Kongōrin-ji　金剛輪寺 ················· *64* D5
Kongōsen-ji (Yata-dera)　金剛山寺(矢田寺) ······ *46* C4
Kongō Station　金剛駅 ················· *51* F6
Kongō-zan　金剛山 ················· *13* G5
Kōnin-ji　弘仁寺 ················· *47* I5
Konkai-kōmyō-ji　金戒光明寺(Kurodani 黒谷) ··· *38* A3
Konohana-ku　此花区 ················· *7* F4
Kōnoike Sports Ground　鴻ノ池運動公園 ··· *48* A4
Kōnoike-shinden Station　鴻ノ池新田駅 ······ *7* H3
Konpuku-ji　金福寺 ················· *40* E2
Konzō-ji　金蔵寺 ················· *10* E6
Kōra-chō　甲良町 ················· *64* D4
Kōrien Station　香里園駅 ················· *7* I2
Kōrigaoka　香里ヶ丘 ················· *7* I1
Kōriyama I.C.　郡山インター ········· *12* D3
Kōriyama Station　郡山駅 ················· *47* F4
Kōro Station　香呂駅 ················· *14* C1
Kōryō-chō　広陵町 ················· *12* E4
Kōryū-ji　幸隆寺 ················· *46* C6
Kōryū-ji　広隆寺 ················· *43* G6
Kosai-shi　湖西市 ················· *55* G6
Kōsan-ji　高山寺 ················· *43* H1
Kōsei-chō　甲西町 ················· *64* C6
Kōshienguchi Station　甲子園口駅 ········· *6* E3
Kōshien Station　甲子園駅 ················· *6* E3
Kōshō-ji　光勝寺(Kūya-dō 空也堂) ········· *35* F5
Kosōan Garden　孤蓬庵庭園 ········· *36* D3
Kōsoku-Nagata Station　高速長田駅 ········· *16* C5
Kōta-chō　幸田町 ················· *54* E5
Kotō-chō　湖東町 ················· *64* D5
Kōtō-in　高桐院 ················· *36* D3
Kōtsū Jinja　交通神社 ················· *38* A5
Kōya-chō　高野町 ················· *9* H7
Kōyaguchi-chō　高野口町 ················· *9* G5
Kōyaguchi Station　高野口駅 ················· *9* G5
Kōya-Ryūjin Q.N.P　高野竜神国定公園 ··· *62* C3
Kōyasan　高野山 ················· *62* D3
Koyasu Kannon　子安観音 ················· *39* F4
Kōyōen Station　甲陽園駅 ················· *6* D2
Koza-chō　古座町 ················· *62* E6
Kozagawa-chō　古座川町 ················· *62* E6
Kozakai-chō　小坂井町 ················· *55* F6
Koza-kyō　古座峡 ················· *62* D6
Kōzan-ji　高山寺 ················· *28* C6
Kōzuno-miya　高津宮 ················· *27* G2
Kudara-dera　百済寺 ················· *64* D5
Kudoyama-chō　九度山町 ················· *9* G6

73

Kuginashi-dō 釘無堂 ·················· 8 E4
Kujō Station (Subway) 九条駅(地下鉄) ·········· 33 G5
Kujōyama Station 九条山駅 ·········· 38 D3
Kujū Station 九条駅 ·················· 47 E3
Kumano-gawa 熊野川 ·················· 63 F5
Kumanogawa-chō 熊野川町 ·········· 62 E5
Kumano-hayatama Jinja 熊野速玉神社 ·········· 62 E5
Kumano Jinja 熊野神社 ·········· 38 A5
Kumanonada-Nigishima Marine Park
    熊野灘二木島海中公園 ·········· 63 F4
Kumanonimasu Jinja 熊野坐神社 ·········· 62 D5
Kumano-shi 熊野市 ·················· 63 F4
Kumatori-chō 熊取町 ·················· 8 D4
Kumatori Station 熊取駅 ·········· 8 D4
Kumeda-ike 久米田池 ·················· 8 E3
Kumeda Station 久米田駅 ·········· 8 E3
Kumihama-chō 久美浜町 ·········· 2 B1
Kumiyama-chō 久御山町 ·········· 11 F5
Kunijima Station 柴島駅 ·········· 22 C2
Kunimi-yama 国見山 ·················· 63 F2
Kurama-dera 鞍馬寺 ·················· 28 A3
Kuramaguchi Station (Subway)
    鞍馬口駅(地下鉄) ·················· 37 G4
Kurama Station 鞍馬駅 ·········· 28 A4
Kurama-yama 鞍馬山 ·················· 10 B4
Kurodashō-chō 黒田庄町 ·········· 4 C1
Kurokawa Station (Subway) 黒川駅(地下鉄) ·········· 56 C4
Kurotaki-mura 黒滝村 ·················· 62 E2
Kurumazaki Jinja 車折神社 ·········· 44 E3
Kurumazaki Station 車折駅 ·········· 44 D3
Kusatsu-shi 草津市 ·················· 64 B6
Kushida-gawa 櫛田川 ·················· 63 G1
Kushimoto-chō 串本町 ·········· 62 D6
Kushimoto Marine Park 串本海中公園 ·········· 62 D7
Kusu-chō 楠町 ·················· 54 B5
Kutsukake I.C. 沓掛インター ·········· 10 D6
Kutsuki-mura 朽木村 ·················· 64 B3
Kuwana-shi 桑名市 ·················· 54 B4
Kuzuha Station 葛葉駅 ·········· 11 G6
Kyōbashi Station 京橋駅 ·········· 25 I1
Kyōbate Station 京終駅 ·········· 47 H3
Kyōshi Station 孝子駅 ·········· 8 A6
Kyōto Central P.O. 京都中央局 ·········· 33 F3
Kyōto City Office 京都市役所 ·········· 35 I4
Kyōto Claft Center 京都クラフトセンター ·········· 38 D6
Kyōto Gokoku Jinja 京都護国神社 ·········· 38 E4
Kyōto-higashi I.C. 京都東インター ·········· 10 D3
Kyōto Int'l Conference Hall 国立京都国際会館 ·········· 40 A5
Kyōto Kaikan 京都会館 ·········· 38 B5
Kyōto-minami I.C. 京都南インター ·········· 10 E5
Kyōto Municipal Art Musm 京都市立美術館 ·········· 38 B4
Kyōto Nat'l Museum 京都国立博物館 ·········· 39 G6

Kyōto Nat'l Mus. of Modern Art
    京都国立近代美術館 ·········· 38
Kyōto Old Palace (Kyōto Gosho) 京都御所 ·········· 35
Kyōto Pref. Library 京都府立図書館 ·········· 38
Kyōto Pref. Med. Coll. 京都府立医大 ·········· 35
Kyōto Pref. Office 京都府庁 ·········· 35
Kyōto Pref. Univ. 京都府立大学 ·········· 37
Kyōto Racecource 京都競馬場 ·········· 29
Kyōto Research Park 京都リサーチパーク ·········· 32
Kyōto-shi 京都市 ·················· 5
Kyōto Station 京都駅 ·········· 33
Kyōto Tower 京都タワー ·········· 33
Kyōto Univ. 京都大学 ·········· 41
Kyōto Univ. Hosp. 京都大学病院 ·········· 41
Kyōto Univ. of Foreign Lang. 京都外国語大学 ·········· 43
Kyūhōji-guchi Station 久宝寺口駅 ·········· 51
Kyūhōji Station 久宝寺駅 ·········· 7

Maihara-chō 米原町 ·················· 64
Maiko Station 舞子駅 ·········· 15
Mainichi Hall 毎日ホール ·········· 23
Maisaka-chō 舞阪町 ·········· 55
Maizuru-shi 舞鶴市 ·········· 3
Makimuku Station 巻向駅 ·········· 12
Makino-chō マキノ町 ·········· 64
Makinoo 槙ノ尾 ·········· 28
Makino Station 牧野駅 ·········· 11
Mangan-ji 満願寺 ·········· 38
Manju-ji 万寿寺 ·········· 39
Manpuku-ji 万福寺 ·········· 29
Manshu-in 曼殊院 ·········· 40
Marine Museum 海洋博物館 ·········· 18
Marunouchi Station (Subway) 丸の内駅(地下鉄) ·········· 58
Marutamachi-bashi (Br.) 丸太町橋 ·········· 38
Marutamachi Station (Subway)
    丸太町駅(地下鉄) ·········· 35
Maruyama Park 円山公園 ·········· 38
Maruyama Station 丸山駅 ·········· 16
Matoya Wan 的矢湾 ·········· 63
Matsubara I.C. 松原インター ·········· 7
Matsubara Jct. 松原ジャンクション ·········· 7
Matsubara-shi 松原市 ·········· 7
Matsugasaki 松ヶ崎 ·········· 40
Matsuhono-ura 松帆の浦 ·········· 15
Matsui-yamate Station 松井山手駅 ·········· 11
Matsuo-dera 松尾寺 ·········· 46
Matsuo Station 松尾駅 ·········· 45
Matsuo Taisha 松尾大社 ·········· 45

tsuo-yama 松尾山 ·········· 45 H4
tsusaka-shi 松阪市 ·········· 63 H1
ya-Futō 摩耶埠頭 ·········· 17 I 3
ya-Ōhashi (Br.) 摩耶大橋 ·········· 19 I 3
ya-san 摩耶山 ·········· 6 B2
iji-mura 明治村 ·········· 54 D2
ijō-kōen Station (Subway)
名城公園駅（地下鉄） ·········· 58 A3
ijō Park 名城公園 ·········· 58 A4
itō-ku 名東区 ·········· 55 I 2
iwa-chō 明和町 ·········· 63 H1
riken Hatoba (American Wharf)
メリケン波止場 ·········· 18 D6
yami Jizō めやみ地蔵 ·········· 38 D6
bu-dera 壬生寺 ·········· 34 D6
doribashi Station (Subway) 緑橋駅（地下鉄） ··· 52 E3
dori-chō 緑町 ·········· 4 B6
dori-ku 緑区 ·········· 55 I 4
doroga-ike 深泥池 ·········· 40 B7
hama-chō 御浜町 ·········· 63 F5
hama-chō 美浜町 ·········· 62 B4
hama-chō 美浜町 ·········· 64 B1
hara-chō 三原町 ·········· 4 A6
hara-chō 美原町 ·········· 9 G1
hara-kita I.C. 美原北インター ·········· 7 H6
hara-minami I.C. 美原南インター ·········· 7 H6
i-dera 三井寺 ·········· 28 E1
kanodai Station 美加の台駅 ·········· 51 F6
kasa Hotsprings Resort 三笠温泉郷 ·········· 48 A1
kasa-yama 三笠山(Wakakusa-yama 若草山) ··· 48 C1
kata-chō 三方町 ·········· 64 B2
kata-chō 美方町 ·········· 2 A1
kawawan Q.N.P. 三河湾国定公園 ·········· 54 D6
kazuki-chō 三日月町 ·········· 2 A3
ki-shi 三木市 ·········· 15 G3
ki-zaki 三木崎 ·········· 63 G4
kkabi-chō 三ヶ日町 ·········· 55 G6
kkaichichō Station 三日市町駅 ·········· 9 G3
kumari Jinja 水分神社 ·········· 62 E2
kunigaoka Station 三国ヶ丘駅 ·········· 7 G6
minashi Station 耳成駅 ·········· 51 I 6
minashi-yama 耳成山 ·········· 13 F3
murodo-ji 三室戸寺 ·········· 29 I 2
nabe-chō 南部町 ·········· 62 B5
nabegawa-mura 南部川村 ·········· 62 B5
nakuchi-chō 水口町 ·········· 64 C6
nami-Chita-chō 南知多町 ·········· 54 D6
namikata Station 南方駅 ·········· 22 C4
nami-ku (Kyōto City) 南区(京都市) ·········· 32 D6
nami-ku (Nagoya City) 南区(名古屋市) ·········· 55 H4
namimorimachi Sta. (Subway)

南森町駅（地下鉄） ·········· 23 I 2
Minami-senba 南船場 ·········· 24 D5
Minami-Senri Station 南千里駅 ·········· 7 G2
Minami-Tatsumi Sta. (Subway) 南巽駅(地下鉄) ··· 52 E5
Minami-yamashiro-mura 南山城村 ·········· 11 H1
Minami-za 南座 ·········· 38 D6
Minatogawa Jinja 湊川神社 ·········· 18 B6
Minatogawa-kōen Sta. (Subway)
湊川公園駅（地下鉄） ·········· 18 A7
Minatogawa Station 湊川駅 ·········· 18 A6
Minato-ku (Nagoya City) 港区(名古屋市) ·········· 55 G4
Minato-ku (Ōsaka City) 港区(大阪市) ·········· 7 F4
Minato-kuyakusho Sta. (Subway)
港区役所駅（地下鉄） ·········· 53 H4
Mineyama-chō 峰山町 ·········· 2 B1
Minokamo-shi 美濃加茂市 ·········· 54 D1
Mino-o-shi 箕面市 ·········· 7 F1
Mino-o Station 箕面駅 ·········· 7 F1
Mino-shi 美濃市 ·········· 3 G1
Minotani Station 箕谷駅 ·········· 6 A2
Mint Bureau 造幣局 ·········· 25 G1
Mirume Jinja 敏馬神社 ·········· 19 J2
Misaki-chō 岬町 ·········· 8 A5
Misaki-kōen Station みさき公園駅 ·········· 8 A5
Misaki Park みさき公園 ·········· 8 A5
Misasagi Station 御陵駅 ·········· 39 F1
Misato-chō 美里町 ·········· 62 C3
Mishima Jinja 三島神社 ·········· 39 G5
Mitake-chō 御嵩町 ·········· 54 E1
Mito-chō 御津町 ·········· 55 F6
Mito Station 弥刀駅 ·········· 51 F4
Mitsu-chō 御津町 ·········· 2 A3
Mitsumine-yama 三峰山 ·········· 8 D5
Miwa-chō 三和町 ·········· 3 B2
Miwa-chō 美和町 ·········· 54 C3
Miwa Station 三輪駅 ·········· 13 E3
Miwa-yama 三輪山 ·········· 12 E2
Miya-gawa 宮川 ·········· 63 I 1
Miyagawa-mura 宮川村 ·········· 63 G2
Miyake-chō 三宅町 ·········· 12 D4
Miyake-hachiman Sta. 三宅八幡駅 ·········· 40 A2
Miyakojima-ku 都島区 ·········· 20 C2
Miyakojima Station (Subway) 都島駅(地下鉄) ··· 20 C2
Miyama-chō 海山町 ·········· 63 F3
Miyama-chō 美山町 ·········· 62 C4
Miyama-chō 美山町 ·········· 3 C2
Miya Spa 三谷温泉 ·········· 55 F6
Miyazu-shi 宮津市 ·········· 3 B1
Miyoshi-chō 三好町 ·········· 54 E4
Mizoguchi Station 溝口駅 ·········· 14 B1
Mizuho-chō 瑞穂町 ·········· 3 C2

Mizuho Ground　瑞穂運動場 ················ *57*　I 1
Mizuho-ku　瑞穂区 ······················· *55*　I 2
Mizukoshi-tōge　水越峠 ····················· *9*　I 3
Mizuma Kannon-dō　水間観音堂 ··········· *8*　D4
Mizuma Station　水間駅 ···················· *8*　E4
Mizunami-shi　瑞浪市 ···················· *55*　F2
Modoribashi　戻り橋 ······················· *37*　F6
Momodani Station　桃谷駅 ················· *27*　I 4
Momoyama-chō　桃山町 ···················· *8*　D7
Momoyama Station　桃山駅 ··············· *29*　H4
Moriguchi-shi　守口市 ······················ *7*　H2
Moriguchi Station (Subway)　守口駅(地下鉄) *52*　E1
Morinomiya Station　森ノ宮駅 ············· *25*　J4
Morishita Station　森下駅 ················· *56*　C3
Moriyama-ku　守山区 ····················· *55*　I 2
Moriyama-shi　守山市 ···················· *64*　B5
Motomachi Station　元町駅 ··············· *18*　D4
Mototanaka Station　元田中駅 ············· *41*　G5
Motoyam Station (Subway)　本山駅(地下鉄) *53*　J2
Mozu Station　百舌鳥駅 ····················· *7*　G6
Mukogawa Station　武庫川駅 ·············· *6*　E3
Mukōmachi Station　向日町駅 ············· *29*　G6
Mukō-shi　向日市 ······················· *29*　G6
Munetada Jinja　宗忠神社 ················· *41*　I 4
Muraoka-chō　村岡町 ······················ *2*　A1
Murin-an Garden　無鄰庵庭園 ············· *38*　B4
Murō-Akame-Aoyama Q.N.P.
　室生赤目青山国定公園 ···················· *63*　F1
Murō-ji　室生寺 ························· *63*　F1
Murō-mura　室生村 ······················· *5*　J4
Mushanokōji-senke Kankyūan
　武者小路千家官休庵 ···················· *37*　F6
Musota Station　六十谷駅 ··················· *8*　B6
Myōen-ji
　妙円寺(Matsigasaki Daikokuten 松ヶ崎大黒天) ·· *40*　C4
Myōhō-in　妙法院 ······················· *39*　G5
Myōhōji Station (Subway)　妙法寺駅(地下鉄) *53*　G6
Myōji Station　妙寺駅 ······················ *9*　F6
Myōkaku-ji　妙覚寺 ····················· *37*　F4
Myōken-ji　妙顕寺 ······················ *37*　F4
Myōondōri Station (Subway)　妙音通駅(地下鉄) *53*　I 4
Myōren-ji　妙蓮寺 ······················· *36*　E4
Myōshin-ji　妙心寺 ······················ *42*　D3
Myōshinji Station　妙心寺駅 ·············· *42*　C3

Nabari-shi　名張市 ························· *5*　J4
Nachi Falls　那智滝 ····················· *62*　E5
Nachikatsuura-chō　那智勝浦町 ············ *62*　E6
Nachi Taisha　那智大社 ·················· *62*　E6
Nachi-zan　那智山 ······················ *62*　E5
Nada-ku　灘区 ···························· *6*　C3
Nada Station　灘駅 ····················· *19*　I 1

Naga-chō　那賀町 ························ *8*
Nagahama-shi　長浜市 ···················· *64*
Nagahara Station (Subway)　長原駅(地下鉄) ····· *53*
Nagahoribashi Sta. (Subway)　長堀橋駅(地下鉄) *24*
Nagai Station　長居駅 ······················ *7*
Nagai Station (Subway)　長居駅(地下鉄) ········· *52*
Nagakute-chō　長久手町 ·················· *54*
Nagano Newtown　長野ニュータウン ··········· *9*
Nagaokakyō-shi　長岡京市 ················ *29*
Nagaoka Tenjin　長岡天神 ················ *29*
Nagaoka-tenjin Station　長岡天神駅 ········· *29*
Nagao Station　長尾駅 ··················· *11*
Nagara-bashi (Br.)　長柄橋 ··············· *22*
Nagara-gawa　長良川 ···················· *54*
Nagara Station　長柄駅 ·················· *12*
Nagase Station　長瀬駅 ·················· *51*
Nagashima-chō　長島町 ·················· *54*
Nagataki Station　長滝駅 ················· *8*
Nagata Station　長田駅 ·················· *16*
Nagata Station (Subway)　長田駅(地下鉄) ······· *16*
Nagata Station (Subway)　長田駅(地下鉄) ······· *53*
Nagoya Castle　名古屋城 ················· *58*
Nagoya City Office　名古屋市役所 ·········· *58*
Nagoyakō Station (Subway)　名古屋港駅(地下鉄) *53*
Nagoya-kyūjōmae Station　ナゴヤ球場前駅 ···· *59*
Nagoya-shi　名古屋市 ···················· *54*
Nagoya Stadium　ナゴヤ球場 ·············· *59*
Nagoya Station　名古屋駅 ················ *58*
Naka-chō　中町 ·························· *4*
Nakafutō Station　中埠頭駅 ··············· *17*
Naka-futō Station　中ふ頭駅 ·············· *50*
Nakagawa-ku　中川区 ···················· *55*
Nakagyō-ku　中京区 ····················· *34*
Nakaheji-chō　中辺路町 ·················· *62*
Nakaiburi Station　中飯降駅 ··············· *9*
Nakakōen Station　中公園駅 ·············· *17*
Naka-ku (Nagoya City)　中区(名古屋市) ······ *59*
Nakamozu Station　中百舌鳥駅 ·············· *9*
Naka-Mozu Station (Subway)
　なかもず駅(地下鉄) ····················· *52*
Nakamura-kōen Station (Subway)
　中村公園駅(地下鉄) ····················· *53*
Nakamura-ku　中村区 ···················· *55*
Nakamura-kuyakusho Sta. (Subway)
　中村区役所駅(地下鉄) ··················· *53*
Nakamura-Nisseki Station (Subway)
　中村日赤駅(地下鉄) ····················· *53*
Nakanoshima　中之島 ···················· *24*
Nakanoshima Park　中之島公園 ············ *24*
Nakatsu-mura　中津村 ··················· *62*
Nakatsu Station (Hankyū Line)　中津駅(阪急線) ·· *23*
Nakatsu Station (Subway)　中津駅(地下鉄) ····· *23*

...ayama-dera　中山寺 ·············· _6_　E1
...ayamadera Station　中山寺駅 ········· _6_　E1
...azakichō Station (Subway)
　...崎町駅(地下鉄) ····················· _23_　G3
...ba City　ナンバシティ ················· _26_　E3
...ba Sports Plaza　難波スポーツプラザ ······ _26_　E4
...ba Station (Nankai Line)　難波駅(南海線) ···· _26_　E3
...ba Station (Subway)　難波駅(地下鉄) ····· _26_　D2
...dan-chō　南淡町 ······················ _4_　A7
...iwa-ku　浪速区 ······················· _26_　C4
...iwa Park　浪速公園 ··················· _26_　C3
...nō-chō　南濃町 ······················· _54_　B3
...sei-chō　南勢町 ······················· _63_　H2
...tō-chō　南島町 ······················· _63_　G2
...zen-in Garden　南禅院庭園 ············· _38_　C2
...zen-ji　南禅寺 ························· _38_　B2
...zen-ji-hōjō Garden　南禅寺方丈庭園 ······ _38_　B2
...abiga-oka　雙ヶ岡 ····················· _42_　D4
...a Dream Land　奈良ドリームランド ······· _48_　A5
...a Nat'l Musm　奈良国立博物館 ·········· _48_　D3
...a Park　奈良公園 ····················· _48_　D2
...a Pref. Art Musm　奈良県立美術館 ······· _48_　C3
...a Pref. Office　奈良県庁 ··············· _48_　C4
...a-shi　奈良市 ························· _47_　F2
...a Station　奈良駅 ····················· _48_　D6
...a Women's Univ.　奈良女子大学 ········· _48_　C4
...ayama Station　平城山駅 ··············· _12_　B3
...uo Station　鳴尾駅 ···················· _6_　E3
...utaki　鳴滝 ·························· _42_　C6
...utaki Station　鳴滝駅 ················· _42_　D5
...shinoki-Jinja　梨木神社 ················ _35_　I1
...te Station　名手駅 ···················· _8_　E6
...'l Bunraku Theater　国立文楽劇場 ········ _27_　F2
...'l Ōsaka Hosp.　国立大阪病院 ··········· _25_　G5
...nbutsu-ji
　念仏寺(Adashino Nenbutsu-ji 化野念仏寺) ··· _44_　B7
...yagawa-shi　寝屋川市 ·················· _7_　H2
...yagawashi Station　寝屋川市駅 ·········· _7_　I2
...uno Station　仁豊野駅 ················· _14_　B2
...atsu-dō　二月堂 ······················ _48_　B2
...non Rhein　日本ライン ················· _54_　D1
...ō Castle　二条城 ····················· _34_　E3
...ō Jinya (Daimyō Lodge)　二条陣屋 ······· _35_　E4
...ō-Ōhashi (Br.)　二条大橋 ··············· _38_　B6
...ō-san　二上山 ························ _13_　E5
...ō Station　二上駅 ···················· _12_　E5
...ō Station　二条駅 ···················· _34_　D4
...na-ji　仁和寺 ······················· _42_　B4
...homaru Garden　二ノ丸庭園 ············ _35_　E3
...ponbashi Station　日本橋駅 ············· _27_　F3
...shiakashi Station　西明石駅 ············ _15_　F6
...shiazai-chō　西浅井町 ················· _64_　C2

Nishidai Park　西代公園 ················· _16_　B6
Nishidai Station　西代駅 ··············· _16_　B6
Nishi-hongan-ji　西本願寺 ·············· _32_　E2
Nishi-kaseda Station　西笠田駅 ·········· _9_　F6
Nishiki-chō　西紀町 ···················· _3_　B2
Nishiki-ichiba　錦市場 ················· _35_　H5
Nishiki Tenmangū　錦天満宮 ············ _35_　H5
Nishi-Kizu Station　西木津駅 ············ _11_　I4
Nishi-ku (Nagoya City)　西区(名古屋市) ···· _55_　H2
Nishi-ku (Ōsaka City)　西区(大阪市) ······ _24_　B5
Nishikujū Station　西九条駅 ············· _21_　F6
Nishikyōgoku Sports Center　西京極運動公園 ···· _43_　J4
Nishikyō-ku　西京区 ··················· _29_　F7
Nishi-motomachi Station　西元町駅 ······· _18_　C6
Nishi-Mukō Station　西向日駅 ··········· _29_　G6
Nishinada Station　西灘駅 ·············· _17_　H2
Nishinagahori Sta. (Subway)　西長堀駅(地下鉄) ···· _24_　A6
Nishinakajima-Minamikata Sta. (Subway)
　西中島南方駅(地下鉄) ··············· _22_　C4
Nishinari-ku　西成区 ··················· _26_　B6
Nishinokyō Station　西ノ京駅 ············ _46_　E3
Nishinomiya I.C.　西宮インター ··········· _6_　E3
Nishinomiya-kitaguchi Station　西宮北口駅 ··· _6_　E2
Nishinomiya-kita I.C.　西宮北インター ······ _6_　C1
Nishinomiya-shi　西宮市 ················ _6_　D3
Nishinomiya Station　西宮駅 ············· _6_　E2
Nishio-shi　西尾市 ····················· _54_　E5
Nishi-Ōtani　西大谷(Ōtani Honbyō 大谷本廟) ···· _39_　F5
Nishi-ōtsu Station　西大津駅 ············ _28_　D1
Nishitakakura Station (Subway)
　西高蔵駅(地下鉄) ·················· _57_　H5
Nishi-Tanabe Station (Subway)
　西田辺駅(地下鉄) ·················· _52_　D6
Nishi-Tawaramoto Station　西田原本駅 ···· _12_　E4
Nishi-Umeda Station (Subway)
　西梅田駅(地下鉄) ·················· _23_　I5
Nishiura Spa　西浦温泉 ················ _54_　E6
Nishiwaki-shi　西脇市 ·················· _4_　B1
Nishi-Yodogawa-ku　西淀川区 ············ _7_　F3
Nishiyoshino-mura　西吉野村 ············ _62_　D2
Nison-in　二尊院 ······················ _44_　C6
Nissay Stadium　日生球場 ·············· _25_　I4
Nisshin-shi　日進市 ··················· _54_　D3
Nittai-ji　日泰寺 ······················ _56_　E1
Niu-Kawakami Jinja　丹生川上神社 ········ _13_　I3
Nodagawa-chō　野田川町 ··············· _2_　B1
Noda-hanshin Station (Subway)
　野田阪神駅(地下鉄) ················ _20_　E6
Noda Station　野田駅 ·················· _20_　E6
Noe-Uchindai Station (Subway)
　野江内代駅(地下鉄) ················ _20_　C1
Nokami-chō　野上町 ··················· _62_　B3

Nomura Art Musm　野村美術館 ·············· *38* B3
Nonomiya Jinja　野宮神社 ················· *44* D5
Nose-chō　能勢町 ······················ *5* E1
Nosegawa-mura　野迫川村 ················ *62* D3
Notogawa-chō　能登川町 ················· *64* C4
Notre-Dame Women's Coll.　ノートルダム女子大学 ·· *37* I1
Nozaki Kannon　野崎観音 ················ *7* I3
Nozaki Station　野崎駅 ·················· *7* I3
Nozato Station　野里駅 ·················· *14* B2
Nukata Station　額田駅 ·················· *51* G3
Nunobiki Falls　布引滝 ·················· *19* E1
Nunobiki Park　布引公園 ················· *18* E1
Nunobiki Tunnel　布引トンネル ············· *18* D1
Nyakuōji Jinja　若王子神社 ··············· *38* B2

Ōbaku Station　黄檗駅 ·················· *29* H3
Obama-shi　小浜市 ···················· *64* A2
Obata-chō　小俣町 ···················· *63* H1
Obitoke-dera　帯解寺 ··················· *47* H4
Obitoke Station　帯解駅 ················· *47* G4
Ōdai-chō　大台町 ····················· *63* G2
Ōdaigahara-zan　大台原山 ················ *63* E3
Ōe-chō　大江町 ······················ *3* B2
Ōe-yama　大江山 ····················· *3* B1
Ōgaki-shi　大垣市 ····················· *54* B2
Ōgimachi Park　扇町公園 ················· *23* H3
Ōgimachi Station (Subway)　扇町駅(地下鉄) ······· *23* H2
Ogoto Spa　雄琴温泉 ··················· *10* B2
Ōguchi-chō　大口町 ···················· *54* D2
Ogura I.C.　巨椋インター ················· *11* F4
Ogura Station　小倉駅 ·················· *29* I3
Ogura-yama　小倉山 ··················· *44* D7
Ōhara　大原 ························· *10* B3
Ōharano Jinja　大原野神社 ··············· *29* G7
Ōi-chō　大飯町 ······················ *3* C1
Oike Station (Subway)　御池駅(地下鉄) ·········· *35* G4
Oinosaka Pass　老ノ坂 ·················· *10* D6
Ōishi Jinja　大石神社 ··················· *29* F3
Oishi-Kōgen　生石高原 ·················· *62* B3
Ōishi Station　大石駅 ··················· *17* I2
Ōji-chō　王子町 ······················ *12* D5
Ōji-kōen Station　王子公園駅 ·············· *17* H1
Ōji Park　王子公園 ···················· *17* H1
Ōji Station　王寺駅 ···················· *12* D5
Oka-dera　岡寺(Ryūgai-ji 竜蓋寺) ··········· *49* H1
Okadera Station　岡寺駅 ················· *13* F3
Ōkawara Station　大河原駅 ··············· *11* H1
Okazaki Betsuin　岡崎別院 ··············· *38* A3
Okazaki Jinja　岡崎神社 ················· *38* A3
Okazaki Park　岡崎公園 ················· *38* B4
Okazaki-shi　岡崎市 ··················· *55* E5

Okino-shima　沖島 ···················· *64*
Ōkōchi-chō　大河内町 ·················· *2*
Ōkōchi Sansō　大河内山荘 ··············· *44*
Ōkubo Station　大久保駅 ················ *15*
Ōkuradani I.C.　大蔵谷インター ············ *15*
Ōkurayama Park　大倉山公園 ············· *18*
Ōkurayama Station (Subway)　大倉山駅(地下鉄) ·· *18*
Ōmi-chō　近江町 ····················· *64*
Ōmi-hachiman-shi　近江八幡市 ············ *64*
Ōmi Jingū　近江神宮 ··················· *28*
Ōmi-Maiko　近江舞子 ·················· *64*
Ōmi-Ōhashi　近江大橋 ·················· *10*
Ōmiwa Jinja　大神神社 ················· *13*
Ōmiya-chō　大宮町 ···················· *63*
Ōmiya-chō　大宮町 ···················· *2*
Ōmiya Station　大宮駅 ·················· *35*
Omuro　御室 ························ *42*
Omuro Station　御室駅 ·················· *42*
Onigajō　鬼ヶ城 ····················· *63*
Onji Station　恩智駅 ··················· *51*
Ōno-chō　大野町 ····················· *54*
Onomachi Station　小野町駅 ·············· *14*
Ono-shi　小野市 ····················· *15*
Onsen-chō　温泉町 ···················· *2*
Oriental Ceramic Musm　東洋陶磁器美術館 ····· *24*
Ōsaka Castle Park　大阪城公園 ············ *25*
Ōsaka Central P.O.　大阪中央局 ··········· *23*
Ōsaka City Office　大阪市役所 ············ *24*
Ōsaka High Court　大阪高裁 ·············· *24*
Ōsaka Int'l Airport　大阪国際空港 ·········· *7*
Ōsakajō-kōen Station　大阪城公園駅 ········· *25*
Ōsakakō Station (Subway)　大阪港駅(地下鉄) ······ *52*
Ōsaka Municipal Univ. (Med.)
　大阪市立大学(医学部) ················ *27*
Ōsaka Pref. Office　大阪府庁 ············· *25*
Ōsaka Castle　大阪城 ·················· *25*
Ōsaka-Sayama-shi　大阪狭山市 ············ *7*
Ōsaka-shi　大阪市 ···················· *5*
Ōsaka Stadium　大阪球場 ··············· *26*
Ōsaka Station　大阪駅 ·················· *23*
Ōsaka Stock Exchange　大阪証券取引所 ······ *24*
Ōsaka Tower　大阪タワー ················ *23*
Ōsaka Univ. (Med.)　大阪大学(医学部) ······· *24*
Ōsaka Univ. Hosp.　大阪大学病院 ·········· *24*
Ōsawano-ike　大沢池 ·················· *44*
Ōsugi Gorge　大杉峡谷 ················· *63*
Ōsu Kannon　大須観音 ················· *59*
Ōsukannon Station (Subway)
　大須観音駅(地下鉄) ················· *59*
Ōsumi Station　大住駅 ·················· *11*
Ōtani Station　大谷駅 ·················· *9*
Ōtani Univ.　大谷大学 ·················· *37*

tsu-Inari Jinja　御辰稲荷神社 ·············· *38* A5
njōga-dake　大天井岳 ························ *62* E2
-mura　大塔村 ······························· *62* C5
-mura　大塔村 ······························· *62* D3
ri Jinja　大鳥神社 ·························· *9* F1
ri Station　鳳駅 ··························· *7* F6
wa-chō　音羽町 ···························· *55* F5
wa-yama　音羽山 ··························· *29* F1
yo Jinja　大豊神社 ························· *38* A2
su I.C.　大津インター ······················ *10* D3
su-shi　大津市 ···························· *10* D2
chiyama-mura　大内山村 ··················· *63* G2
da-chō　大宇陀町 ························· *13* F1
ariasahi-shi　尾張旭市 ····················· *54* D3
ase-shi　尾鷲市 ··························· *63* F3
a-chō　大屋町 ····························· *2* A2
amazaki-chō　大山崎町 ····················· *11* F5
odo-chō　大淀町 ··························· *13* H4
aki Station　尾崎駅 ······················· *8* B4
ne Station　大曽根駅 ······················ *56* C2
ne Station (Subway)　大曽根駅(地下鉄) ······ *56* C2

arl Farm　真珠養殖場 ······················ *63* I2
arl Island　真珠島 ························· *63* I1
npon-yama　ポンポン山 ···················· *10* E6
t Island　ポートアイランド ················· *17* H5
t Terminal Station　ポートターミナル駅 ······· *19* G6
t Tower　ポートタワー ····················· *18* D6

gō-in　来迎院 ····························· *39* I5
kushi-sha　落柿舎 ························· *44* C6
kan-ji　霊鑑寺 ···························· *41* J2
un-in　霊雲院 ····························· *39* I6
nge-ji　蓮華寺 ···························· *42* B4
kan-Den'entoshi Station　林間田園都市駅 ······ *13* H6
kyū-ji　林丘寺 ···························· *40* C1
sen-ji　臨川寺 ···························· *44* E4
sumeikan Univ.　立命館大学 ················ *36* A4
tō-chō　栗東町 ···························· *64* B6
tō I.C.　栗東インター ······················ *10* D1
kkaku-dō　六角堂 ························· *35* G4
kō Island　六甲アイランド ·················· *6* C3
kō Marine Park　六甲マリンパーク ··········· *6* C3
kōmichi Station　六甲道駅 ················· *17* J1
kō-san　六甲山 ···························· *6* C2
kō Tunnel　六甲トンネル ··················· *18* B2
kubanchō Station (Subway)　六番町駅(地下鉄) *57* I6
kudō-chinnō-ji　六道珍皇寺 ················ *39* E6
kuharamitsu-ji　六波羅蜜寺 ················ *33* I1
kuō-in　鹿王院 ···························· *44* D4

Rokuōin Station　鹿王院駅 ················· *44* D3
Rozan-ji　盧山寺 ··························· *35* I1
Ruins of Akasaka Castle　赤坂城跡 ········· *9* H3
Ruins of Arai Barrier　新居関跡 ············ *55* G7
Ruins of Asuka-inafuchi Palace　飛鳥稲渕宮跡 *49* J2
Ruins of Asuka-itabuki Palace　伝飛鳥板蓋宮跡 ··· *49* H3
Ruins of Asuka-kiyomigahara Palace
　飛鳥浄御原宮跡 ························· *49* F3
Ruins of Azuchi Castle　安土城跡 ·········· *64* C5
Ruins of Chihaya Castle　千早城跡 ········· *9* H4
Ruins of Gangōji Tower　元興寺塔跡 ········ *48* E4
Ruins of Heian Palace　平安宮内裏跡 ······· *34* D2
Ruins of Heijō Place　平城宮跡 ············ *47* F1
Ruins of Ikedaya　池田屋跡 ··············· *35* I4
Ruins of Kawara-dera　川原寺跡 ··········· *49* H3
Ruins of Nagahama Castle　長浜城跡 ······· *64* D3
Ruins of Nagaoka Palace　長岡京跡 ········ *29* G6
Ruins of Naniwa Palace　難波宮跡 ········· *25* H4
Ruins of Odani Castle　小谷城跡 ··········· *64* D2
Ruins of Sai-ji　西寺跡 ··················· *32* C4
Ruins of Shigaraki Palace　紫香楽宮跡 ······ *64* C6
Ruins of Toyura-dera　豊浦寺跡 ············ *49* F4
Ruins of Yamashiro-Kokubun-ji　山城国分寺跡 *11* H3
Ryōan-ji　竜安寺 ·························· *42* A3
Ryōan-ji Garden　竜安寺庭園 ·············· *42* A4
Ryōanjimichi Sta.　竜安寺道駅 ············· *42* C3
Ryōtoku-ji　了徳寺(Daikondaki-dera 大根焚寺) · *42* B6
Ryōzen Kannon　霊山観音 ················· *38* E5
Ryūhon-ji　立本寺 ························· *36* C6
Ryūjin-mura　竜神村 ······················ *62* C4
Ryūjin Spa　竜神温泉 ····················· *62* C4
Ryūmon-dake　竜門岳 ····················· *13* G2
Ryūō-chō　竜王町 ························· *64* C5
Ryūsen-ji　竜泉寺 ························· *55* I2

Saga　嵯峨 ······························· *44* E3
Sagano　嵯峨野 ··························· *44* E2
Saga Arashiyama Station　嵯峨嵐山駅 ······· *44* D4
Sagimori Jinja　鷺森神社 ·················· *40* C2
Saidai-ji　西大寺 ························· *46* E1
Saidai-ji　西大寺 ························· *38* E5
Saigyō-an　西行庵 ························ *45* I4
Saihō-ji (Koke-dera)　西芳寺(苔寺) ········· *34* B5
Saiin Station　西院駅 ····················· *36* D5
Saimyō-ji　西明寺 ························ *37* H5
Sainokamino-yashiro　幸神社 ·············· *58* E2
Sakaemachi Station　栄町駅 ··············· *59* E2
Sakae Station (Subway)　栄駅(地下鉄) ······· *59* E2
Sakahogi-chō　坂祝町 ····················· *54* D1
Sakai-higashi Station　堺東駅 ············· *7* G5
Sakai-kita I.C.　堺北インター ··············· *7* G7
Sakai-minami I.C.　堺南インター ············· *9* F2

79

Sakai-shi　堺市 ……………………………… 7 F6
Sakaishi Station　堺市駅 ………………… 7 G5
Sakaisuji-honmachi Sta. (Subway)
　堺筋本町駅（地下鉄）………………… 24 E4
Sakamoto Station　坂本駅 ……………… 28 C1
Sakishima　先志摩 ………………………… 63 I 2
Sakuragawa Station (Subway)　桜川駅（地下鉄）…… 26 C2
Sakurai-shi　桜井市 ……………………… 13 F2
Sakurai Station　桜井駅 ………………… 13 F3
Sakurajima Station　桜島駅 ……………… 7 F4
Sakuranomiya-bashi (Br.)　桜の宮橋 …… 25 G1
Sakyō-ku　左京区 ………………………… 40 D2
Sanadayama Park　真田山公園 ………… 27 I 2
Sanage-yama　猿投山 …………………… 54 E3
Sandanpeki　三段壁 ……………………… 62 B6
Sanda-shi　三田市 ………………………… 4 D2
Sangane-san　三ヶ根山 ………………… 54 E6
Sangatsu-dō　三月堂（Hokke-dō 法華堂）… 48 B2
Sangō-chō　三郷町 ……………………… 12 D5
San-in Kaigan N.P.　山陰海岸国立公園 … 2 A1
Sanjōga-take　山上ヶ岳 ………………… 62 E2
Sanjōguchi Station　三条口駅 ………… 34 C4
Sanjō-ōhashi (Br.)　三条大橋 ………… 38 C6
Sanjō Station　三条駅 …………………… 35 I 4
Sanjō Station　三条駅 …………………… 38 C6
Sanjūsangen-dō
　三十三間堂（Renge-ōin 蓮華王院）… 39 G6
Sannan-chō　山南町 ……………………… 4 D1
Sannen-zaka　産寧坂 …………………… 39 E5
Sannomiya Center-gai　三宮センター街 … 18 E4
Sannomiya Jinja　三宮神社 …………… 18 E4
Sannomiya Station　三宮駅 …………… 19 F3
Santō-chō　山東町 ……………………… 64 E3
Santō-chō　山東町 ………………………… 2 B2
Sanyō-Himejihigashi I.C.　山陽姫路東インター … 14 C2
Sanyō-Himejinishi I.C.　山陽姫路西インター …… 14 A2
Sanzen-in　三千院 ……………………… 28 A2
Saori-chō　佐織町 ……………………… 54 B3
Sarusawano-ike　猿沢池 ………………… 48 D4
Sasayama-chō　篠山町 …………………… 4 D1
Saya-chō　佐屋町 ………………………… 54 B3
Sayama Station　狭山駅 ………………… 9 G2
Sayama-yūenmae Station　狭山遊園前駅 … 9 G2
Sefuku-ji　施福寺 ………………………… 9 F4
Seidan-chō　西淡町 ……………………… 4 A6
Seifūsō Garden　清風荘庭園 …………… 41 H6
Seigan-ji　誓願寺 ……………………… 35 I 5
Seiganto-ji　青岸渡寺 …………………… 62 E5
Seika-chō　精華町 ……………………… 11 H4
Seikan-ji　清閑寺 ……………………… 39 G3
Seiryō-ji　清涼寺（Saga Shakadō 嵯峨釈迦堂）… 44 C5
Seishin-chūō Station　西神中央駅 …… 15 G5

Seiwa-mura　勢和村 ……………………… 63
Seki-chō　関町 …………………………… 64
Sekigahara-chō　関ヶ原町 ……………… 54
Sekikō-ji　石光寺 ………………………… 13
Sekime Station (Subway)　関目駅（地下鉄）… 52
Sekinomiya-chō　関宮町 ………………… 2
Seki-shi　関市 …………………………… 54
Sekiya Station　関屋駅 ………………… 12
Sekizan-zen-in　赤山禅院 ……………… 40
Senba-chūō　船場中央 …………………… 24
Senbayashi-Ōmiya Sta. (Subway)
　千林大宮駅（地下鉄）………………… 52
Senboku Newtown　泉北ニュータウン … 9
Senda Station　千旦駅 …………………… 8
Sengenchō Station (Subway)　浅間町駅（地下鉄）… 58
Senkō-ji　千光寺（Daihikaku 大悲閣）… 44
Sennan I.C.　泉南インター ………………… 8
Sennan-shi　泉南市 ……………………… 8
Sennichimae-dōri　千日前通り ………… 26
Sennyū-ji　泉涌寺 ……………………… 39
Sen-oku Hakkokan Musm　泉屋博古館 … 38
Senrioka Station　千里丘駅 ……………… 7
Senriyama　千里山 ……………………… 7
Seta-higashi I.C.　瀬田東インター ……… 10
Setonaikai N.P.　瀬戸内海国立公園 …… 2
Seto-shi　瀬戸市 ………………………… 54
Settsu-minami I.C.　摂津南インター ……… 7
Settsu-Motoyama Station　摂津本山駅 … 6
Settsu-shi　摂津市 ………………………… 7
Settsu-Tonda Station　摂津富田駅 ……… 7
Shakaga-dake　釈迦ヶ岳 ………………… 62
Shakudo Station　尺土駅 ……………… 13
Shakuzō-ji　石像寺（Kuginuki Jizō 釘抜地蔵）… 36
Shichiri-mihama　七里御浜 ……………… 63
Shiga-chō　志賀町 ……………………… 64
Shiga-hondōri Station (Subway)
　志賀本通駅（地下鉄）………………… 56
Shigaraki-chō　信楽町 …………………… 64
Shigatsu-dō　四月堂 …………………… 48
Shigino Station　鴫野駅 ………………… 7
Shigisan　信貴山 ………………………… 12
Shigisanguchi Station　信貴山口駅 …… 7
Shijōnawate Jinja　四條畷神社 ………… 7
Shijōnawate-shi　四條畷市 ……………… 7
Shijōnawate Station　四條畷駅 ………… 7
Shijō-ōhashi　四条大橋 ………………… 38
Shijō-Ōmiya Station　四条大宮駅 …… 34
Shijō Station　四条駅 …………………… 35
Shijō Station (Subway)　四条駅（地下鉄）… 35
Shikama　飾磨 …………………………… 14
Shiki Station　志紀駅 …………………… 7
Shima-chō　志摩町 ……………………… 63

mamoto-chō　島本町 ················ *11* F6
manouchi　島之内 ················ *24* E6
minhiroba Station　市民広場駅 ··········· *17* G6
mizu-chō　清水町 ················ *62* C3
mizu Station　清水駅 ··············· *58* B1
moda Station　下田駅 ·············· *12* E5
mogamo　下鴨 ·················· *40* E6
mogoryō Jinja　下御霊神社 ··········· *35* H3
mogyō-ku　下京区 ················ *33* F1
mohyōgo Station　下兵庫駅 ··········· *13* I 6
moichi-chō　下市町 ··············· *13* H3
moichiguchi Station　下市口駅 ·········· *13* H3
moisaka Station　下井阪駅 ··········· *8* D6
mo-Kitayama-mura　下北山村 ·········· *62* E4
mokoma Station　下狛駅 ············· *11* H4
momatsu Station　下松駅 ············ *8* E3
motsu-chō　下津町 ··············· *62* B3
n-asahi-chō　新旭町 ··············· *64* C3
nden Station　新田駅 ·············· *29* J3
nfukae Station (Subway)　新深江駅(地下鉄) ··· *52* E4
nge Station　新家駅 ·············· *8* C4
ngū-chō　新宮町 ················ *2* A3
ngū-shi　新宮市 ················· *62* E5
n-Hie Jinja　新日吉神社 ············· *39* G5
n-Imamiya Station　新今宮駅 ·········· *26* E6
n-Ishikiri Station　新石切駅 ·········· *51* G3
njō-chō　新庄町 ················· *13* F4
nkaichi Station　新開地駅 ··········· *18* A7
n-Kanaoka Sta. (Subway)　新金岡駅(地下鉄) ··· *52* D7
nkawa-chō　新川町 ··············· *54* C3
n-Kōbe Station　新神戸駅 ············ *19* F1
nkyōku　新京極 ················· *35* H5
nmei Jinja　神明神社 ·············· *35* H6
n Moriyama Station　新守山駅 ········· *56* B1
n-Nagata Station　新長田駅 ··········· *16* B6
n-nyodō
如堂(Shinshōgokuraku-ji 真正極楽寺) ···· *41* I 3
nobugaoka Station　忍ヶ丘駅 ·········· *7* I 2
nodayama Station　信太山駅 ·········· *7* F7
n-Ōmiya Station　新大宮駅 ··········· *47* G2
n-Ōsaka Station　新大阪駅 ··········· *22* B4
npuku-ji　新福寺 ················ *57* H1
nsaibashi Station (Subway)
斉橋駅(地下鉄) ················· *24* D6
nsen-en　神泉苑 ················ *35* E3
nshiro-shi　新城市 ··············· *55* G5
nshō-ji　神照寺 ················· *64* D3
n-Yakushi-ji　真薬師寺 ············· *48* E1
n-zaike Station　新在家駅 ··········· *17* J1
ogamaguchi Sta. (Subway)　塩釜口駅(地下鉄) ·· *53* I 3

Shiomibashi Station　汐見橋駅 ········· *26* B2
Shiono-misaki　潮岬 ·············· *62* D7
Shioya Station　塩屋駅 ············· *15* H6
Shippō-chō　七宝町 ··············· *54* C3
Shippōryū-ji　七宝竜寺 ············· *8* D5
Shirahama-chō　白浜町 ············· *62* B5
Shirahama Spa　白浜温泉 ············ *62* B5
Shirahige Jinja　白鬚神社 ············ *64* B4
Shirakawa Park　白川公園 ············ *59* F4
Shiramine Jingū　白峯神宮 ··········· *37* F5
Shirasaki Coast　白崎海岸 ··········· *62* A4
Shiromi　城見 ·················· *25* I 2
Shisen-dō　詩仙堂(Jōzan-ji 丈山寺) ······· *40* E2
Shishigatani　鹿ヶ谷 ·············· *41* I 2
Shitennō-ji　四天王寺 ·············· *27* G5
Shitennōjimae Sta. (Subway)
四天王寺前駅(地下鉄) ············· *27* G4
Shiyakusho Station (Subway)　市役所駅(地下鉄) *58* C3
Shizumi Station　志染美駅 ··········· *12* E5
Shōchiku Movie Studio　松竹撮影所 ······ *43* F7
Shōfuku-ji　祥福寺 ··············· *16* D3
Shōgo-in　聖護院 ················ *38* A5
Shōgun-zuka　将軍塚 ·············· *38* D4
Shōgyō-in　正行院(Saru-dera 猿寺) ······ *33* G3
Shōhō-ji　正法寺 ················ *38* E4
Shōji Station (Subway)　小路駅(地下鉄) ···· *52* E5
Shōjōke-in　清浄華院 ·············· *35* I 1
Shōkoku-ji　相国寺 ··············· *37* G5
Shōmyō-ji　称名寺 ··············· *48* C5
Shōnai-dōri Station (Subway)　庄内通駅(地下鉄) ·· *56* B6
Shōnai Greens　庄内緑地 ············ *56* A6
Shōnai-ryokuchi-kōen Sta. (Subway)
庄内緑地公園駅(地下鉄) ············ *56* A6
Shōnen-ji　称念寺(Neko-dera 猫寺) ······ *36* D4
Shōren-in　青蓮院 ··············· *38* C4
Shōren-in Dainichidō　青蓮院大日堂 ······ *38* E4
Shōrin-ji　正林寺 ················ *39* G5
Shōryaku-ji　正暦寺 ·············· *47* J4
Shōsei-en Garden　渉成園(Kikoku-tei 枳殻邸) ····· *33* G2
Shoshazan Enkyō-ji　書写山円教寺 ······ *14* A1
Shōsō-in　正倉院 ················ *48* B3
Shōwachō Station (Subway)　昭和町駅(地下鉄) ·· *52* D6
Shōwa-ku　昭和区 ··············· *55* H3
Shuchiin Coll.　種智院大学 ··········· *32* D4
Shūgakuin Imperial Villa　修学院離宮 ····· *40* B1
Shūgakuin Station　修学院駅 ·········· *40* C3
Shukugawa Station　夙川駅 ··········· *10* A6
Shūzan　周山 ·················· *54* C2
Sobue-chō　祖父江町 ·············· *54* B2
Sōgōundō-kōen Station (Subway)
総合運動公園駅(地下鉄) ············ *53* G6
Sokujō-in　即成院 ··············· *33* J4

Sone Station　曽根駅 ································· 14　C3
Sonezaki　曽根崎 ································· 23　I4
Sonezaki-shinchi　曽根崎新地 ············ 23　I5
Sonobe-chō　園部町 ······················· 3　C2
Sōrin-ji　雙林寺 ···························· 38　D4
Sōzenji Station　崇禅寺駅 ················ 22　B2
Ssiin　西院 ································· 43　G2
Ssiin Kasuga Jinja　西院春日神社 ······ 43　G2
Suda Station　隅田駅 ····················· 13　I6
Suga-jima　菅島 ····························· 63　I1
Suga Jinja　須賀神社 ······················ 38　A5
Sugawara Jinja　菅原神社 ·················· 46　E2
Sugimotochō Station　杉本町駅 ·········· 7　G5
Suita I.C.　吹田インター ··················· 7　G1
Suita-shi　吹田市 ·························· 7　G2
Suita Station　吹田駅 ······················ 7　G2
Suma I.C.　須磨インター ···················· 15　H6
Suma-ku　須磨区 ···························· 15　H6
Suma Station　須磨駅 ······················ 15　H6
Suminodō Station　住道駅 ················· 7　I3
Suminoe-kōen Sta. (Subway)
　住之江公園駅(地下鉄) ··············· 52　B7
Suminoe-ku　住之江区 ····················· 7　F5
Sumiya　角屋 ······························· 32　D2
Sumiyoshi-ku　住吉区 ····················· 7　G5
Sumiyoshi Station　住吉駅 ················· 6　C3
Sumiyoshi Taisha　住吉大社 ··············· 7　F5
Sumiyoshi-taisha Station　住吉大社駅 ····· 50　D5
Sōrakuen Garden　相楽園 ·················· 18　C4
Susami-ch4o　すさみ町 ··················· 62　C6
Suwayama Park　諏訪山公園 ··············· 18　C3
Suzuka Circuit　鈴鹿サーキット ········· 54　A5
Suzuka Q.N.P.　鈴鹿国定公園 ············ 3　E3
Suzuka-shi　鈴鹿市 ························ 54　A5
Suzuka-tōge　鈴鹿峠 ······················ 64　E7
Suzurandai Station　鈴蘭台駅 ············· 15　I5

Tachibana-dera　橘寺 ····················· 49　H3
Tachibana Station　立花駅 ················· 6　E3
Tadaoka-chō　忠岡町 ····················· 8　E2
Tadaoka Station　忠岡駅 ·················· 8　E2
Tado-chō　多度町 ·························· 54　B3
Taga-chō　多賀町 ·························· 64　D4
Taga Taisha　多賀大社 ····················· 64　D4
Tahara-chō　田原町 ························ 55　F7
Taiji-chō　太地町 ·························· 62　E6
Taikō-an　退耕庵 ·························· 39　I6
Taima-chō　当麻町 ························· 13　F5
Taima-dera　当麻寺 ························ 13　F5
Taimadera Station　当麻寺駅 ·············· 13　E5
Taishibashi-Imaichi Sta. (Subway)
　太子橋今市駅(地下鉄) ················ 52　E1

Taishi-chō　太子町 ························ 2
Taishi-chō　太子町 ························ 9
Taishōgun-hachi Jinja　大将軍八神社 ······ 36
Taishō-ku　大正区 ························· 21
Taishō Station　大正駅 ···················· 26
Tajimi-shi　多治見市 ······················ 54
Tajiri-chō　田尻町 ························· 8
Takabata Station (Subway)　高畑駅(地下鉄) ··· 53
Takagamine　鷹峰 ·························· 36
Takahama-chō　高浜町 ····················· 3
Takahama-shi　高浜市 ····················· 54
Takaida Station (Subway)　高井田駅(地下鉄) ·· 53
Takaishi-shi　高石市 ······················ 7
Takamado-yama　高円山 ···················· 47
Takamatsuzuka Old Mound　高松塚古墳 ···· 49
Takami-yama　高見山 ······················ 63
Takano　高野 ······························· 40
Takao　高雄 ································· 28
Takaoguchi Station　高雄口駅 ·············· 42
Takaraga-ike　宝ヶ池 ······················ 40
Takaragaike Park　宝ヶ池公園 ·············· 40
Takaragaike Station　宝ヶ池駅 ············· 40
Takarazuka I.C.　宝塚インター ············· 6
Takarazuka-shi　宝塚市 ···················· 6
Takarazuka Station　宝塚駅 ················ 6
Takasago-shi　高砂市 ······················ 14
Takashima-chō　高島町 ···················· 64
Takashino-hama Station　高師浜駅 ········· 8
Takatomi-chō　高富町 ····················· 54
Takatori-chō　高取町 ······················ 13
Takatori Station　鷹取駅 ·················· 16
Takatori-yama　高取山 ····················· 13
Takatsuki-chō　高月町 ····················· 64
Takatsuki-shi　高槻市 ····················· 7
Takayama　高山 ···························· 12
Takayasu Station　高安駅 ·················· 51
Takayasu-yama　高安山 ····················· 12
Takayasu-yama Station　高安山駅 ·········· 51
Takebe Taisha　建部大社 ··················· 64
Takeisao Jinja　建勲神社 ··················· 36
Takeminawake Jinja　建水分神社 ··········· 9
Take-shima　多景島 ························· 64
Taketoyo-chō　武豊町 ····················· 54
Taki-chō　多気町 ·························· 63
Takiguchi-dera　滝口寺 ···················· 44
Takihata Dam　滝畑ダム ··················· 9
Takino-chō　滝野町 ························· 4
Takino Station　滝野駅 ···················· 15
Takino-Yashiro I.C.　滝野社インター ······· 15
Takitani Station　滝谷駅 ··················· 51
Takojizō Station　蛸地蔵駅 ················ 8
Tako-yakushi　鮹薬師 ······················ 35

made Station　玉手駅 ················· 13　G4
made Station (Subway)　玉出駅(地下鉄) ··· 52　B6
magawa Station (Subway)　玉川駅(地下鉄) ···· 63　H1
maki-chō　玉城町 ····················· 25　I 6
matsukuri Station　玉造駅 ············· 48　C1
mukeyama Jinja　手向山神社 ··········· 11　G4
nabe-chō　田辺町 ···················· 62　C5
nabe-shi　田辺市 ···················· 11　G4
nabe Station　田辺駅 ················· 52　D6
nabe Station (Subway)　田辺駅(地下鉄) ··· 52　D6
nagawa Station　多奈川駅 ············· 8　A5
naka　田中 ························· 41　G5
nakami-yama　田上山(Tagami-yama 太神山) ··· 11　E1
nbabashi Station　丹波橋駅 ············ 3　C2
nba-chō　丹波町 ···················· 32　C1
nbaguchi Station　丹波口駅 ············ 2　B1
ngo-chō　丹後町 ···················· 2　B1
nimachi-kyūchōme Sta. (Subway)
谷町九丁目駅(地下鉄) ··············· 27　G3
nimachi-rokuchōme Sta. (Subway)
谷町六丁目駅(地下鉄) ··············· 25　G6
nimachi-yonchōme Sta. (Subway)
谷町四丁目駅(地下鉄) ··············· 25　G4
nnowa Station　淡輪駅 ··············· 8　A5
ntō-chō　但東町 ···················· 2　B1
nzan Jinja　談山神社 ················· 13　F2
rui-chō　垂井町 ····················· 54　A2
rui Station　樽井駅 ················· 8　C4
rumi-ku　垂水区 ···················· 15　G6
rumi Station　垂水駅 ················· 15　G6
tsuno-shi　竜野市 ··················· 2　A3
tsuta Taisha　竜田大社 ··············· 12　D5
waramoto-chō　田原本町 ·············· 12　E3
waramoto Station　田原本駅 ··········· 12　E3
njin-bashi (Br.)　天神橋 ·············· 25　F2
njinbashisuji-rukuchōme Sta.
天神橋筋六丁目駅 ··················· 23　G2
njin-zaki　天神崎 ··················· 62　B5
nju-an　天授庵 ····················· 38　C3
nkawa-mura　天川村 ················· 62　E2
nma-bashi (Br.)　天満橋 ·············· 25　F2
nmabashi Station　天満橋駅 ··········· 25　F2
nmachō Station (Subway)　伝馬町駅(地下鉄) ··· 57　J4
nman-gū　天満宮 ··················· 23　I 2
nma Station　天満駅 ················· 23　H2
nnōji-ku　天王寺区 ·················· 27　G5
nnōji Park　天王寺公園 ··············· 27　F6
nnōji Station　天王寺駅 ·············· 27　G7
nnōji Station (Subway)　天王寺駅(地下鉄) ··· 27　G6
nnō-zan　天王山 ···················· 11　F6
npaku-ku　天白区 ··················· 55　I 3
nri I.C.　天理インター ··············· 12　D3

Tenrikyō H.Q.　天理教本部 ············ 12　D2
Tenri-shi　天理市 ··················· 12　D3
Tenri Station　天理駅 ················ 12　D3
Tenryū-ji　天竜寺 ··················· 44　E5
Tenryū-shi　天竜市 ·················· 55　I 5
Teradachō Station　寺田町駅 ·········· 27　H7
Toa Road　トアロード ··············· 18　D3
Tobakaidō Station　鳥羽街道駅 ········· 33　H6
Toba-shi　鳥羽市 ··················· 63　I 1
Tōbushijōmae Station　東部市場前駅 ····· 7　G4
Tochū-goe　途中越 ·················· 10　A4
Tōdai-ji　東大寺 ··················· 48　C2
Tōei Uzumasa Movie Village　東映太秦映画村 ··· 42　E5
Tōfuku-ji　東福寺 ··················· 33　I 5
Tōfuku-ji　東福寺 ··················· 39　J6
Tōfukuji Station　東福寺駅 ············ 33　H4
Toga-Mikita Station　栂・美木多駅 ······ 9　F2
Togan-ji　渡岸寺 ··················· 64　D2
Toganoo　栂ノ尾 ··················· 28　C6
Togetsu-kyō (Br.)　渡月橋 ············· 44　E5
Tōgō-chō　東郷町 ·················· 54　D4
Tōin-chō　東員町 ··················· 54　B4
Tō-ji　東寺(Kyōōgokoku-ji 教王護国寺) ····· 32　D4
Tōji-in　等持院 ···················· 36　A5
Tōjiin Station　等持院駅 ·············· 36　A6
Tōjō-chō　東条町 ··················· 15　H1
Tōkaidōri Station (Subway)　東海通駅(地下鉄) ··· 53　H4
Tōkai-shi　東海市 ··················· 54　D4
Toki-shi　土岐市 ··················· 55　E2
Tokiwa　常盤 ······················ 42　D5
Tokiwa Station　常盤駅 ·············· 42　D6
Tōkō-ji　東光寺 ···················· 15　H2
Tokoname-shi　常滑市 ··············· 54　C5
Tokuan Station　徳庵駅 ·············· 7　H3
Tokugawa-en　徳川園 ··············· 56　D2
Tokushō-ji　徳照寺 ················· 18　B5
Tomio Station　富雄駅 ··············· 51　H3
Tomoga-shima　友ヶ島 ·············· 4　C6
Tondabayashi-shi　富田林市 ··········· 7　H7
Tonoki Station　富木駅 ·············· 7　F6
Torahime-chō　虎姫町 ··············· 64　D3
Toribeyama Cemetery　鳥辺山墓地 ······ 39　F4
Tōsenji Spa　湯泉地温泉 ·············· 62　E4
Tōshi-jima　答志島 ················· 63　H1
Tōshōdai-ji　唐招提寺 ··············· 47　F2
Totsu-kawa　十津川 ················· 62　D4
Totsukawa-mura　十津川村 ··········· 62　D4
Totsukawa Spa　十津川温泉 ··········· 62　D4
Tottorinoshō Station　鳥取ノ荘駅 ······· 8　B5
Toyoake-shi　豊明市 ················ 54　D4
Toyohashi-shi　豊橋市 ··············· 55　F6
Toyokawa Inari　豊川稲荷 ············ 55　G6

83

Toyokawa-shi　豊川市 ················ 55　F6
Toyokuni Jinja　豊国神社 ············ 39　G6
Toyonaka I.C.　豊中インター ········· 7　F2
Toyonaka-shi　豊中市 ················ 7　F2
Toyonaka Station　豊中駅 ············ 7　F2
Toyono-chō　豊能町 ················· 5　F2
Toyooka-shi　豊岡市 ················ 2　A1
Toyosato-chō　豊郷町 ··············· 64　D4
Toyota-shi　豊田市 ················· 54　E4
Trade Center　産業貿易展示館 ········· 19　F5
Traditional Industry Hall　伝統産業会館 ··· 38　B5
Tsubaki Spa　椿温泉 ················ 62　C6
Tsubosaka-dera　壺坂寺 ·············· 13　G3
Tsubosakayama Station　壺坂山駅 ······· 13　G3
Tsuchiyama-chō　土山町 ·············· 64　D6
Tsuchiyama Station　土山駅 ··········· 14　E5
Tsuda Station　津田駅 ··············· 7　J1
Tsufuro Dam　津風呂ダム ············· 13　H2
Tsukaguchi Station　塚口駅 ··········· 7　E2
Tsukijiguchi Station (Subway)　築地口駅(地下鉄) 53　H4
Tsukimiyama Station　月見山駅 ········· 16　A7
Tsukuno Station　津久野駅 ············ 7　F6
Tsumori Station　津守駅 ·············· 26　A6
Tsuna-chō　津名町 ·················· 4　B5
Tsuruga-shi　敦賀市 ················ 64　C1
Tsurugi Jinja　剣神社 ··············· 39　H5
Tsuruhashi Sta. (Subway)　鶴橋駅(地下鉄) ·· 27　I3
Tsuruhashi Station　鶴橋駅 ··········· 27　J3
Tsurumai Station　鶴舞駅 ············· 59　H1
Tsurumi-ku　鶴見区 ················· 7　H3
Tsurumi-ryokuchi Sta. (Subway)
　鶴見緑地駅(地下鉄) ··············· 52　E2
Tsu-shi　津市 ····················· 54　A6
Tsushima-shi　津島市 ················ 54　B3
Tsūten-kaku　通天閣 ················ 27　E5
Tsutsui-Hachiman Jinja　筒井八幡神社 ····· 19　H1
Tsutsui Station　筒井駅 ·············· 46　E6

Uchita-chō　打田町 ················· 8　D6
Uchita Station　打田駅 ·············· 8　D6
Ueda Station (Subway)　植田駅(地下鉄) ··· 53　I3
Uehonmachi Station　上本町駅 ········· 27　H3
Ueno-shi　上野市 ··················· 5　J3
Uenoshiba Station　上野芝駅 ·········· 7　F6
Uhō-in　雨宝院(Nishijin Shōten 西陣聖天) · 36　E5
Uji-gawa　宇治川 ··················· 11　F5
Ujigawa Rhein　宇治川ライン ·········· 11　F3
Uji Jinja　宇治神社 ················· 29　I2
Uji-shi　宇治市 ···················· 29　I3
Uji Station　宇治駅 ················· 29　I3
Ujitawara-chō　宇治田原町 ············ 11　G3

Ukimi-dō　浮御堂 ·················· 10　E
Ukyō-ku　右京区 ··················· 42　E
Umeda　梅田 ····················· 23　I
Umekōji Steam Locomotive Musm
　梅小路蒸気機関車館 ·············· 32　C
Umenomiya Taisha　梅宮大社 ·········· 45　C
Umezu　梅津 ····················· 45　G
Unebi Station　畝傍駅 ··············· 13　F
Unebi-yama　畝傍山 ················· 13　F
Uneme Jinja　妥女神社 ··············· 48　E
Unryū-in　雲龍院 ·················· 39
Uozumi Station　魚住駅 ·············· 14
Uryū-yama　瓜生山 ················· 41
Ushitakisan Daiitoku-ji　牛滝山大威徳寺 ··· 8
Utano-chō　菟田野町 ················ 5
Utsubo Park　靭公園 ················ 24　E
Uzumasa　太秦 ···················· 43
Uzumasa Station　太秦駅 ············· 43
Uzumasa-yasui　太秦安井 ············· 42

Wachi-chō　和知町 ················· 3　C
Wada-misaki　和田岬 ················ 6
Wadamisaki Station　和田岬駅 ········· 16
Wadayama-chō　和田山町 ············· 2
Wakae-Iwata Station　若江岩田駅 ······· 51　C
Wakakusa-yama　若草山(Mikasa-yama 三笠山) · 48
Wakamiya Hachiman (Nagoya)
　若宮八幡(名古屋) ··············· 59　C
Wakamiya Hachimangū　若宮八幡宮 ······ 39
Wakanoura　和歌ノ浦 ················ 62
Wakasawan Q.N.P.　若狭湾国定公園 ······ 3
Wakayama Castle　和歌山城 ··········· 8
Wakayama I.C.　和歌山インター ········ 8
Wakayama-shi　和歌山市 ············· 8
Wakayamashi Station　和歌山市駅 ······· 8
Wakayama Station　和歌山駅 ·········· 8
Wakigami Station　掖上駅 ············ 13
Wanishita Jinja　和爾下神社 ··········· 47
Wanouchi-chō　輪之内町 ············· 54
Wara Tenjin　わら天神 ·············· 36
Watarai-chō　度会町 ················ 63
Wazuka-chō　和束町 ················ 11

Yabachō Station (Subway)　矢場町駅(地下鉄) · 59　C
Yabu-chō　養父町 ·················· 2
Yachiyo-chō　八千代町 ··············· 4
Yaenosato Station　八戸ノ里駅 ········· 51
Yagi-chō　八木町 ·················· 5
Yagoto Station (Subway)　八事駅(地下鉄) ·· 53
Yagyū　柳生 ····················· 12
Yakujin Station　厄神駅 ·············· 14
Yakuno-chō　夜久野町 ··············· 2

akushi-ji　薬師寺 ･････････････････ 47　F3
amanakadani Spa　山中渓温泉 ････ 8　C5
amanakadani Station　山中渓駅 ･･･ 8　C5
amanomachi Station　山の街駅 ･･･ 6　A2
amanouchi　山ノ内 ･･････････････ 43　G3
amanouchi Station　山ノ内駅 ･････ 34　A4
amashina-ku　山科区 ･････････････ 29　F2
amashina Station　山科駅 ････････ 29　E2
amashiro-chō　山城町 ････････････ 11　H3
amate Station (Subway)　やまて駅(地下鉄) ･････ 18　D4
amato-Futami Station　大和二見駅 ･･･ 13　I5
amato-gawa　大和川 ･･･････････････ 7　E5
amato-Kamiichi Station　大和上市駅 ･･ 13　H3
amato-Koizumi Station　大和小泉駅 ･･ 46　D6
amato-Kōriyama-shi　大和郡山市 ･･ 46　D4
amato-Saidaiji Station　大和西大寺駅 ･ 47　E1
amato-Shinjō Station　大和新庄駅 ･･ 13　F4
amato-Takada-shi　大和高田市 ････ 13　F4
amato-Takada Station　大和高田駅 ･ 13　E4
amato-Yagi Station　大和八木駅 ･･･ 13　F3
amazaki-chō　山崎町 ･･････････････ 2　A3
amazaki Station　山崎駅 ･･･････････ 29　I7
anagimoto Station　柳本駅 ･･･････ 12　E3
anaizu-chō　柳津町 ･･･････････････ 54　B2
ao Airport　八尾空港 ･･･････････････ 7　H5
ao I.C.　八尾インター ･･･････････････ 7　H4
ao-minami Station (Subway)　八尾南駅(地下鉄) 53　F7
ao-shi　八尾市 ･･･････････････････････ 7　H5
ao Station　八尾駅 ･･･････････････････ 7　H5
aotsu-chō　八百津町 ･･･････････････ 54　E1
asaka-chō　弥栄町 ･･･････････････････ 3　B1
asaka Jinja　八坂神社 ･･･････････････ 38　D5
asaka Tower　八坂の塔(Hōkan-ji 法観寺) ･･････ 38　E5
ashiro-chō　社町 ･･･････････････････ 15　F1
ashirochō Station　社町駅 ･･･････････ 15　E1
asu-chō　野洲町 ･････････････････････ 64　B5
asui Konpiragū　安井金比羅宮 ･･････ 38　E6
asutomi-chō　安富町 ･･･････････････ 2　A2
ata-dera　矢田寺 ･･･････････････････ 35　H4
atomi-chō　弥富町 ･････････････････ 54　C4
awata-shi　八幡市 ･････････････････ 11　F5
awatashi Station　八幡市駅 ･･･････ 29　I6
odo-gawa　淀川 ･･･････････････････ 7　F3
odogawa-ku　淀川区 ･･･････････････ 22　B6
odogawa-ōhashi (Br.)　淀川大橋 ･･ 20　D6
odogawa Station　淀川駅 ･･･････････ 20　D6
odo Station　淀駅 ･･････････････････ 29　I5
odoyabashi Station (Subway)
　淀屋橋駅(地下鉄) ･･･････････････ 24　C2
ōgen-in　養源院 ･･･････････････････ 39　G6
ogo-chō　余呉町 ･･･････････････････ 64　C2
ōka-chō　八鹿町 ･････････････････････ 2　A2

Yōkaichi-shi　八日市市 ･･･････････ 64　D5
Yokawa-chō　吉川町 ･･･････････････ 15　H2
Yokawa Chūdō　横川中堂 ･･････････ 10　B3
Yokawa I.C.　吉川インター ････････ 15　H1
Yokawa Jct.　吉川ジャンクション ･･･ 15　I1
Yokkaichi-shi　四日市市 ･･･････････ 54　B4
Yōrō-chō　養老町 ･･･････････････････ 54　A2
Yōrō Falls　養老ノ滝 ･･･････････････ 54　A2
Yoshida　吉田 ･･･････････････････････ 41　I5
Yoshida Jinja　吉田神社 ･･･････････ 41　I4
Yoshida Station　吉田駅 ･･･････････ 51　G3
Yoshida-yama　吉田山 ･･･････････････ 41　H4
Yoshiki-en　吉城園 ･･･････････････････ 48　C3
Yoshiminosato Station　吉見ノ里駅 ･･･ 8　C4
Yoshino-chō　吉野町 ･･･････････････ 13　H2
Yoshinoguchi Station　吉野口駅 ･･･ 13　G4
Yoshino Jingū　吉野神宮 ･･･････････ 13　H3
Yoshino-Jingū Station　吉野神宮駅 ･･ 13　H2
Yoshino-Kumano N.P.　吉野熊野国立公園 ･･････ 62　E3, E6
Yoshino Station　吉野駅 ･･･････････ 13　H3
Yoshino-yama　吉野山 ･･･････････････ 62　E2
Yotsubashi Station (Subway)　四ッ橋駅(地下鉄) ･･ 24　C6
Yuasa-chō　湯浅町 ･･･････････････････ 62　B4
Yukawa Spa　湯川温泉 ･･･････････････ 4　A1
Yumesaki-chō　夢前町 ･･･････････････ 62　D5
Yunomine Spa　湯ノ峰温泉 ･･････････ 62　D5
Yunoyama Spa　湯ノ山温泉 ･･････････ 54　A4
Yura-chō　由良町 ･･･････････････････ 40　B5
Yūsen-ji　湧泉寺 ･･･････････････････ 40　B5
Yūzaki Station　結崎駅 ･･･････････････ 12　D4

Zaō-dō　蔵王堂 ･･･････････････････ 13　H2
Zenjō-ji　禅定寺 ･･･････････････････ 11　F3
Zenpō-ji　善峰寺 ･･･････････････････ 10　E6
Zensui-ji　善水寺 ･･･････････････････ 64　C6

Government Offices
官公庁

① Prefectural Offices (*Fuchō* 府庁, *Kenchō* 県庁)

Kyōto Fuchō 京都府庁	075-451-8111
Ōsaka Fuchō 大阪府庁	06-941-0351
Aichi Kenchō 愛知県庁	052-961-2111
Gifu Kenchō 岐阜県庁	0582-72-1111
Hyōgo Kenchō 兵庫県庁	078-341-7711
Mie Kenchō 三重県庁	0592-24-3070
Nara Kenchō 奈良県庁	0742-22-1101
Shiga Kenchō 滋賀県庁	0775-24-1121
Wakayama Kenchō 和歌山県庁	0734-32-4111

② City Offices (*Shiyakusho* 市役所)

Kōbe 神戸	078-331-8181
Kyōto 京都	075-222-3111
Nagoya 名古屋	052-961-1111
Ōsaka 大阪	06-208-8181
Aioi 相生	07912-3-7111
Akashi 明石	078-912-1111
Amagasaki 尼崎	06-489-6880
Anjō 安城	0566-76-1111
Arida 有田	0737-83-1111
Ashiya 芦屋	0797-31-2121
Ayabe 綾部	0773-42-3280
Bisai 尾西	0586-62-8111
Chiryū 知立	0566-83-1111
Daitō 大東	0720-72-2181
Ena 恵那	0573-26-2111
Fujiidera 藤井寺	0729-39-1111
Fukuchiyama 福知山	0773-22-6111
Gamagōri 蒲郡	0533-66-1111
Gifu 岐阜	058-265-4141
Gobō 御坊	0738-22-4111
Gose 御所	07456-2-3001
Habikino 羽曳野	0729-58-1111
Hekinan 碧南	0566-41-3311
Hamakita 浜北	053-587-3111
Hamamatsu 浜松	053-457-2111
Handa 半田	0569-21-3111

Hannan 阪南	0724-71-5678
Hashima 羽島	058-392-1111
Hashimoto 橋本	0736-33-1111
Higashiōsaka 東大阪	0729-62-1331
Hikone 彦根	0749-22-1411
Himeji 姫路	0792-21-2111
Hirakata 枚方	0720-41-1221
Hisai 久居	0592-55-3110
Ibaraki 茨木	0726-22-8121
Ichinomiya 一宮	0586-73-9111
Ikeda 池田	0727-52-1111
Ikoma 生駒	07437-4-1111
Inazawa 稲沢	0587-32-1111
Inuyama 犬山	0568-61-1800
Ise 伊勢	0596-23-1111
Itami 伊丹	0727-83-1234
Iwakura 岩倉	0587-66-1111
Iwata 磐田	0538-32-2111
Izumi 和泉	0725-41-1551
Izumiōtsu 泉大津	0725-33-1131
Izumisano 泉佐野	0724-63-1212
Jōyō 城陽	07745-2-1111
Kadoma 門真	06-902-1231
Kainan 海南	0734-82-4111
Kaizuka 貝塚	0724-23-2151
Kakamigahara 各務原	0583-83-1111
Kakogawa 加古川	0794-24-1151
Kameoka 亀岡	0771-22-3131
Kameyama 亀山	05958-2-1111
Kani 可児	0574-62-1111
Kariya 刈谷	0566-23-1111
Kasai 加西	0790-42-1111
Kashiba 香芝	07457-6-2001
Kashihara 橿原	07442-2-4001
Kashiwara 柏原	0729-72-1501
Kasugai 春日井	0568-81-5111
Katano 交野	0720-92-0121
Kawachinagano 河内長野	0721-53-1111
Kawanishi 川西	0727-40-1111

Name	Tel.	Name	Tel.
shiwada 岸和田	0724-23-2121	Suzuka 鈴鹿	0593-82-1100
maki 小牧	0568-72-2101	Tajimi 多治見	0572-22-1111
nan 江南	0587-54-1111	Takahama 高浜	0566-52-1111
sai 湖西	053-576-1111	Takaishi 高石	0722-65-1001
mano 熊野	05978-9-4111	Takarazuka 宝塚	0797-71-1141
satsu 草津	0775-63-1234	Takasago 高砂	0794-42-2101
wana 桑名	0594-24-1136	Takatsuki 高槻	0726-74-7111
aizuru 舞鶴	0773-62-2300	Tanabe 田辺	0739-22-5300
atsubara 松原	0723-34-1550	Tatsuno 龍野	0791-63-3131
atsusaka 松阪	0598-53-4322	Tenri 天理	07436-3-1001
ki 三木	0794-82-2000	Tenryū 天竜	0539-26-1111
no 美濃	0575-33-1122	Toba 鳥羽	0599-25-1111
nokamo 美濃加茂	0574-25-2111	Tōkai 東海	0562-33-1111
no-o 箕面	0727-23-2121	Toki 土岐	0572-54-1111
yaza 宮津	0772-22-2121	Tokoname 常滑	0569-35-5111
zunami 瑞浪	0574-25-2111	Tondabayashi 富田林	0721-25-1000
riguchi 守口	06-992-1221	Toyoake 豊明	0562-92-1111
riyama 守山	0775-83-2525	Toyohashi 豊橋	0532-51-2421
ukō 向日	075-931-1111	Toyokawa 豊川	05338-9-2111
abari 名張	0595-63-2111	Toyonaka 豊中	06-858-2525
agahama 長浜	0749-62-4111	Toyooka 豊岡	0796-23-1111
agaokakyō 長岡京	075-951-2121	Toyota 豊田	0565-31-1212
akatsugawa 中津川	0573-66-1111	Tsu 津	0592-26-1231
ara 奈良	0742-34-1111	Tsuruga 敦賀	0770-21-1111
eyagawa 寝屋川	0720-24-1181	Tsushima 津島	0567-24-1111
shinomiya 西宮	0798-35-3151	Ueno 上野	0595-21-4111
shio 西尾	0563-56-2111	Uji 宇治	0774-22-3141
shiwaki 西脇	0795-22-3111	Wakayama 和歌山	0734-32-0001
ama 小浜	0770-53-1111	Yamatokōriyama 大和郡山	07435-3-1151
ou 大府	0562-47-2111	Yamatotakada 大和高田	0745-22-1101
gaki 大垣	0584-81-4111	Yao 八尾	0729-91-3881
kazaki 岡崎	0564-23-6495	Yōkaichi 八日市	0748-24-1234
mihachiman 近江八幡	0748-33-3111	Yokkaichi 四日市	0593-51-1155
no 小野	0794-63-1000		
sakasayama 大阪狭山	0723-66-0011		
tsu 大津	0775-23-1234		
wariasahi 尾張旭	0561-53-2111		
wase 尾鷲	05972-2-1111		
akai 堺	0722-33-1101		
akurai 桜井	07444-2-9111		
anda 三田	0795-63-1111		
eki 関	0575-22-3131		
ennan 泉南	0724-83-0001		
eto 瀬戸	0561-82-7111		
ettsu 摂津	06-383-1111		
hijōnawate 四條畷	0720-77-2121		
hingū 新宮	0735-22-5231		
hinshiro 新城	05362-3-1111		
uita 吹田	06-384-1231		
umoto 洲本	0799-22-3321		

③ Ward Offices (Kuyakusho 区役所)

〔ŌSAKA 大阪〕

Abeno 阿倍野	06-621-1421
Asahi 旭	06-952-3121
Chūō 中央	06-264-8500
Fukushima 福島	06-462-1441
Higashinari 東成	06-972-1212
Higashisumiyoshi 東住吉	06-629-7321
Higashiyodogawa 東淀川	06-327-1031
Hirano 平野	06-702-3331
Ikuno 生野	06-717-1121
Jōtō 城東	06-932-1351
Kita 北	06-362-1300
Konohana 此花	06-462-1331
Minato 港	06-572-5251
Miyakojima 都島	06-352-1221

Naniwa 浪速	06-633-1101	Shōwa 昭和	052-731-15*
Nishi 西	06-538-7301	Tenpaku 天白	052-803-11*
Nishinari 西成	06-659-1121		
Nishiyodogawa 西淀川	06-472-1241		
Suminoe 住之江	06-683-1234		
Sumiyoshi 住吉	06-692-1161		
Taishō 大正	06-553-3311		
Tennōji 天王寺	06-772-1131		
Tsurumi 鶴見	06-913-1111		
Yodogawa 淀川	06-301-1241		

〔KYŌTO 京都〕

Fushimi 伏見	075-611-1101
Higashiyama 東山	075-561-1191
Kamigyō 上京	075-441-0111
Kita 北	075-432-1181
Minami 南	075-681-3111
Nakagyō 中京	075-812-0061
Nishikyō 西京	075-381-7121
Sakyō 左京	075-771-4211
Shimogyō 下京	075-371-7101
Ukyō 右京	075-861-1101
Yamashina 山科	075-592-3050

〔KŌBE 神戸〕

Chūō 中央	078-232-4411
Higashinada 東灘	078-841-4131
Hyōgo 兵庫	078-511-2111
Kita 北	078-593-1111
Nada 灘	078-871-5101
Nagata 長田	078-691-5121
Nishi 西	078-929-0001
Suma 須磨	078-731-4341
Tarumi 垂水	078-708-5151

〔NAGOYA 名古屋〕

Atsuta 熱田	052-681-1431
Chikusa 千種	052-762-3111
Higashi 東	052-935-2271
Kita 北	052-911-3131
Meitō 名東	052-773-1111
Midori 緑	052-621-2111
Minami 南	052-811-5161
Minato 港	052-651-3251
Mizuho 瑞穂	052-841-1521
Moriyama 守山	052-793-3434
Naka 中	052-241-3601
Nakagawa 中川	052-362-1111
Nakamura 中村	052-451-1241
Nishi 西	052-521-5311

Hotels and Inns
ホテル，旅館

〔KYŌTO CITY　京都市〕

ANA H. Kyōto　京都全日空ホテル	075-231-1155
H. Alpha Kyōto　ホテルアルファ京都	075-241-2000
H. Fujita Kyōto　ホテルフジタ京都	075-222-1511
H. Ginmondo　ホテルギンモンド	075-221-4111
H. Hokke Club Kyōto	
ホテル法華クラブ京都店	075-361-1251
Hieizan Kokusai Kankō H.	
比叡山国際観光ホテル	075-701-2111
H. Keihan Kyōto　ホテル京阪京都	075-661-0321
H. New Kyōto　ホテルニュー京都	075-801-2111
H. Nikkō Princes Kyōto	
ホテル日航プリンセス京都	075-342-2410
H. Oaks Kyōto-Shijō	
ホテルオークス京都四条	075-371-0941
Holiday inn Kyōto　ホリディ・イン京都	075-721-3131
H. Rich Kyōto　ホテルリッチ京都	075-669-3400
H. Sanflower Kyōto　ホテルサンフラワー京都	075-761-9111
H. Sunroute Kyōto　ホテルサンルート京都	075-371-3711
Karasuma Kyōto H.　からすま京都ホテル	075-371-0111
Kyōto Brighton H.　京都ブライトンホテル	075-441-4411
Kyōto Central Inn　京都セントラル・イン	075-211-1666
Kyōto Century H.　京都センチュリーホテル	075-351-0111
Kyōto City H.　京都シティホテル	075-431-7161
Kyōto Garden H.　京都ガーデンホテル	075-255-2000
Kyōto Gion H.　京都祇園ホテル	075-551-2111
Kyōto Grand H.　京都グランドホテル	075-341-2311
Kyōto H.　京都ホテル	075-211-5111
Kyōto Kokusai H.　京都国際ホテル	075-222-1111
Kyōto Palaceside H.	
京都パレスサイドホテル	075-431-8171
Kyōto Park H.　京都パークホテル	075-525-3111
Kyōto Prince H.　京都プリンスホテル	075-781-4141
Kyōto Royal H.　京都ロイヤルホテル	075-223-1234
Kyōto Shin-Hankyū H.　京都新阪急ホテル	075-343-5300
Kyōto Takaragaike Prince H.	
京都宝ヶ池プリンスホテル	075-712-1111
Kyōto Tōkyū H.　京都東急ホテル	075-341-2411
Kyōto Tōkyū Inn　京都東急イン	075-593-0109

Kyōto Tower H.　京都タワーホテル	075-361-3211
Kyōto Tower H. No. 2　京都第二タワーホテル	075-361-3261
Kyōto Tower H. No. 3　京都第三タワーホテル	075-343-3111
Miyako Hotel　都ホテル	075-771-7111
New Miyako H.　新都ホテル	075-661-7111
Sanjō-Karasuma H. Kyōto	
三条烏丸ホテル京都	075-256-3331
Sun H. Kyōto　サンホテル京都	075-241-3351
Urban H. Kyōto　アーバンホテル京都	075-647-0606

〔ŌTSU CITY　大津市〕

Biwako Grand H.　琵琶湖グランドホテル	0775-79-2111
Biwako H.　琵琶湖ホテル	0775-24-1511
Biwako Ishiyama H.　びわこ石山ホテル	0775-33-0660
H. New Saichi　ホテルニューサイチ	0775-43-2511
Ōtsu Prince H.　大津プリンスホテル	0775-21-1111
Royal Oak H.　ロイヤルオークホテル	0775-43-0111

〔MORIYAMA CITY　守山市〕

H. Biwako Plaza　ホテルびわ湖プラザ	0775-85-4111
H. Lake Biwa　ホテルレークビワ	0775-85-2511
Laforet Biwako　ラフォーレ琵琶湖	0775-85-3811

〔HIKONE CITY　彦根市〕

Hikone Prince H.　彦根プリンスホテル	0749-26-1111
H. Ōmi Plaza　近江プラザホテル	0749-22-2111
H. Sunroute Hikone　ホテルサンルート彦根	0749-26-0123

〔NAGAHAMA CITY　長浜市〕

Nagahama Royal H.　長浜ロイヤルホテル	0749-64-2000

〔ŌSAKA CITY　大阪市〕

ANA H. Ōsaka　大阪全日空ホテル	06-347-1112
Ark H. Ōsaka　アークホテル大阪	06-252-5111
Asahi Plaza H. Sennichimae	
朝日プラザホテル千日前	06-211-1011
Business H. Kikuei　ビジネスホテルきくえい	06-633-5656
Business H. Nissei　ビジネスホテルニッセイ	06-632-8111
Center H. Ōsaka　センターホテル大阪	06-223-1600

Chisan H. Shin-Ōsaka チサンホテル新大阪	06-302-5571	Ōsaka Green H. 大阪グリーンホテル	06-532-1091
Chisan H. Shinsaibashi チサンホテル心斉橋	06-263-1511	Ōsaka Hilton 大阪ヒルトン	06-347-7111
City Route H. シティルートホテル	06-448-1000	Ōsaka Kokusai H. 大阪コクサイホテル	06-941-2661
East H. イーストホテル	06-364-1151	Ōsaka Kōrakuen H. 大阪後楽園ホテル	06-251-2111
H. Consort ホテルコンソルト	06-304-1511	Ōsaka Riverside H.	
H. Do Sports Plaza		大阪リバーサイドホテル	06-928-3251
ホテルドゥスポーツプラザ	06-245-3311	Ōsaka Shanpia H. 大阪シャンピアホテル	06-312-5151
H. Echo Ōsaka ホテルエコー大阪	06-633-1141	Ōsaka Teikoku H. 大阪帝国ホテル	06-211-8151
H. Granvia Ōsaka ホテルグランヴィア大阪	06-344-1235	Ōsaka Tōkyū H. 大阪東急ホテル	06-373-2411
H. Hanshin ホテル阪神	06-344-1661	Ōsaka Tōkyū Inn 大阪東急イン	06-315-0109
H. Kansai ホテル関西	06-312-7971	Park H. パークホテル	06-444-0809
H. Keihan Ōsaka ホテル京阪大阪	06-945-0321	Plaza Ōsaka プラザオーサカ	06-303-1000
H. Kurebe Umeda ホテルくれべ梅田	06-361-7201	Royal H. ロイヤルホテル	06-448-1121
H. Mitsufu ホテルミツフ	06-304-5171	Shin-Ōsaka Sen-i City H.	
H. Nankai-Nanba ホテル南海なんば	06-649-1521	新大阪センイシティーホテル	06-394-3331
N. NCB ホテルNCB	06-443-2255	Shin-Ōsaka Sun Plaza H.	
H. New Ōtani Ōsaka		新大阪サンプラザホテル	06-350-1111
ホテルニューオータニ大阪	06-941-1111	Shin-Ōsaka Washington H.	
H. Nikkō Ōsaka ホテル日航大阪	06-244-1111	新大阪ワシントンホテル	06-303-8111
H. Oaks Shin-Ōsaka ホテルオークス新大阪	06-302-5141	Sunny-stone H. サニーストンホテル	06-390-0001
Hokke Club Ōsaka 法華クラブ大阪	06-313-3171	Tennōji Miyako H. 天王寺都ホテル	06-779-1501
Holiday Inn Nankai Ōsaka		Tennōji Tōei H. 天王寺東映ホテル	06-775-2121
ホリディイン南海大阪	06-213-8281	Tōkō H. 東興ホテル	06-363-1201
H. Ōsaka World ホテル大阪ワールド	06-361-1100	Tōyō H. 東洋ホテル	06-372-8181
H. Plaza ホテルプラザ	06-453-1111	Umeda OS H. 梅田OSホテル	06-312-1271
H. Sun Life ホテルサンライフ	06-443-1231		
H. Sunroute Umeda ホテルサンルート梅田	06-373-1111	〔TOYONAKA CITY 豊中市〕	
H. Sun White ホテルサンホワイト	06-942-3711	H. Airport Fuji ホテルエアポートふじ	06-843-8811
H. The Luther ホテル ザ・ルーテル	06-942-2281	H. A.P ホテルエービー	06-843-2561
Lions H. Ōsaka ライオンズホテル大阪	06-201-1511	H. Ivory ホテルアイボリー	06-849-1111
Mitsui Garden H. Ōsaka		Ōsaka Airport H. 大阪エアーポートホテル	06-855-4621
三井ガーデンホテル大阪	06-223-1131	Senri Hankyū H. 千里阪急ホテル	06-872-2211
Mitsui Urban H. Ōsaka			
三井アーバンホテル大阪	06-374-1111	〔IKEDA CITY 池田市〕	
Mitsui Urban H. Ōsaka Baytower		H. Kurebe Kūkō ホテルくれべ空港	06-843-7201
三井アーバンホテル大阪ベイタワー	06-577-1111		
Miyako H. Ōsaka 都ホテル大阪	06-773-1111	〔SUITA CITY 吹田市〕	
Nakanoshima Inn 中之島イン	06-447-1122	Esaka Tōkyū Inn 江坂東急イン	06-338-0109
New Hankyū H. 新阪急ホテル	06-372-5101	H. Daitō ホテルダイトー	06-338-5121
New Hankyū H. Annex		H. Parkside ホテルパークサイド	06-386-9191
新阪急ホテルアネックス	06-372-5101	Sunny Stone H. サニーストンホテル	06-386-0001
New Oriental H. ニューオリエンタルホテル	06-538-7141	Sunny Stone H. NO. 2	
New Ōsaka H. ニュー大阪ホテル	06-305-2345	第二サニーストンホテル	06-386-3200
New Shinsaibashi H. ニュー心斉橋ホテル	06-251-3711		
Ōsaka Castle H. 大阪キャッスルホテル	06-942-2401	〔MORIGUCHI CITY 守口市〕	
Ōsaka Corona H. 大阪コロナホテル	06-323-3151	Moriguchi Prince H. 守口プリンスホテル	06-994-1111
Ōsaka Dai-ichi H. 大阪第一ホテル	06-341-4411	Dainichi Terminal H. 大日ターミナルホテル	06-900-1111
Ōsaka Fujiya H. 大阪富士屋ホテル	06-211-5522		
Ōsaka Garden Palace 大阪ガーデンパレス	06-396-6211	〔KADOMA CITY 門真市〕	
Ōsaka Grand H. 大阪グランドホテル	06-202-1212	Kadoma Public H. 門真パブリックホテル	06-906-1151

〔SAKAI CITY　堺市〕				
ty H. Seiunsō　シティホテル青雲荘	0722-41-4545		Green Hill H. Akashi	
Liberty Plaza　ホテルリバティプラザ	0722-32-2211		グリーンヒルホテル明石	078-912-0111
Nankai Sakai　ホテル南海さかい	0722-33-7111		H. Castle Plaza　ホテルキャッスルプラザ	078-927-1111
Sun Plaza　ホテルサンプラザ	0722-22-6633			
Sunroute Sakai　ホテルサンルート堺	0722-32-0303		**〔HIMEJI CITY　姫路市〕**	

Hotel	Phone		Hotel	Phone
nkai H.　臨海ホテル	0722-47-1111		H. Himeji Plaza　ホテル姫路プラザ	0792-81-9000
			Himeji Castle H.　姫路キャッスルホテル	0792-84-3311
〔ZUMISANO CITY　泉佐野市〕			Himeji Green H.　姫路グリーンホテル	0792-89-0088
rport Inn Prince			Himeji Washington H.　姫路ワシントンホテル	0792-25-0111
エアーポートインプリンス	0724-63-2211		H. Okuuchi　ホテルオクウチ	0792-22-8000
rst H.　ファーストホテル	0724-62-0011		H. Sun Garden Himeji	
oliday Inn Kansaikūkō			ホテルサンガーデン姫路	0792-22-2231
ホリディ・イン関西空港	0724-69-1112		H. Sunroute Himeji　ホテルサンルート姫路	0792-85-0811
New Yutaka　ホテルニューユタカ	0724-61-2950			
			〔NARA CITY　奈良市〕	
〔KISHIWADA CITY　岸和田市〕			Business H. New Takatsuji	
ty H. Bellsimon　シティホテルベルシモン	0724-39-2121		ビジネスホテルニューたかつじ	0742-34-5371
			H. Fujita Nara　ホテルフジタ奈良	0742-23-8111
〔KŌBE CITY　神戸市〕			H. Sunroute Nara　ホテルサンルート奈良	0742-22-5151
hisan H. Kōbe　チサンホテル神戸	078-341-8111		Nara City H.　奈良シティホテル	0742-34-4600
een Hill H. (No. 1)			Nara H.　奈良ホテル	0742-26-3300
グリーンヒルホテル（第一）	078-222-1221		Nara Royal　奈良ロイヤルホテル	0742-34-1131
een Hill H. (No. 2)			Nara Three M H.　奈良スリーエムホテル	0742-33-5656
グリーンヒルホテル（第二）	078-222-0909			
Mizukami　ホテル水上	078-575-5871		**〔WAKAYAMA CITY　和歌山市〕**	
Sunroute Kōbe　ホテルサンルート神戸	078-578-0500		Daiichi Fuji H.　第一富士ホテル	0734-31-3351
obe Gajōen H.　神戸雅叙園ホテル	078-341-0301		Mitsui Urban H. Wakayama	
obe Harborland New Ōtani			三井アーバンホテル和歌山	0734-32-1111
神戸ハーバーランドニューオータニ	078-360-1111		Tōei Inn Wakayama　東映イン和歌山	0734-23-1081
obe Plaza H.　神戸プラザホテル	078-332-1141		Wakayama Terminal H.	
obe Portpier H.　神戸ポートピアホテル	078-302-1111		和歌山ターミナルホテル	0734-25-3333
obe Tōkyū Inn　神戸東急イン	078-291-0109		Wakayama Tōkyū Inn　和歌山東急イン	0734-32-0109
obe Washington H.				
神戸ワシントンホテル	078-331-6111		**〔SHIRAHAMA　白浜〕**	
okkō Oriental H.　六甲オリエンタルホテル	078-891-0333		Chisan H. Shirahama　チサンホテル白浜	0739-42-4343
okkōsan H.　六甲山ホテル	078-891-0301		H. Green Hill Shirahama	
ain-Kōbe Oriental H.			ホテルグリーンヒル白浜	0739-42-2733
新神戸オリエンタルホテル	078-291-1121		Shirarasō Grand H.　白良荘グランドホテル	0739-43-0100
unside H.　サンサイドホテル	078-232-3331			
			〔NACHI-KATSUURA　那智勝浦〕	
〔AKARAZUKA CITY　宝塚市〕			H. Urashima　ホテル浦島	07355-2-1011
akarazuka H.　宝塚ホテル	0797-87-1151		Katsuura City Plaza Resort H.	
			勝浦シティプラザリゾートホテル	07355-2-6600
〔ITAMI CITY　伊丹市〕				
ami Daiichi H.　伊丹第一ホテル	0727-77-0111		**〔NAGOYA CITY　名古屋市〕**	
			Business H. Inaho　ビジネスホテル稲穂	052-451-1281
〔AKASHI CITY　明石市〕			Chisan H. Nagoya　チサンホテル名古屋	052-452-3211
kashi Castle H.　明石キャッスルホテル	078-913-1551		Chisan H. Nagoya-sakae	
kashi Luminous H.　明石ルミナスホテル	078-928-1177		チサンホテル名古屋栄	052-962-2411
			City H. Nagoya　シティホテル名古屋	052-452-6223

Daiichi Fuji H. 第一富士ホテル	052-452-1111	
Daini Fuji H. 第二富士ホテル	052-931-1111	
Ekimae Mont Blanc H. 駅前モンブランホテル	052-541-1121	
Fushimi Mont Blanc H. 伏見モンブランホテル	052-232-1121	
H. Castle Plaza ホテルキャッスルプラザ	052-582-2121	
H. Chiyoda ホテルチヨダ	052-221-6711	
H. Kiyoshi Nagoya ホテルキヨシ名古屋	052-321-5663	
H. Nagoya Castle ホテルナゴヤキャッスル	052-521-2121	
H. Palace Nagoya ホテルパレス名古屋	052-452-6151	
H. Sunroute Nagoya ホテルサンルート名古屋	052-571-2221	
Kanayama Plaza H. 金山プラザホテル	052-331-6411	
Lions H. Nagoya ライオンズホテル名古屋	052-211-6511	
Lions Plaza Nagoya ライオンズプラザ名古屋	052-241-1500	
Meitetsu Grand H. 名鉄グランドホテル	052-582-2211	

Meitetsu New Grand H.
名鉄ニューグランドホテル　052-452-5511

Nagoya Central H. 名古屋セントラルホテル	052-203-5511
Nagoya Crown H. 名古屋クラウンホテル	052-211-6633
Nagoya Daiichi H. 名古屋第一ホテル	052-581-4411

Nagoya Daini Washington H.
名古屋第二ワシントンホテル　052-962-7111

Nagoya Fuji Park H. 名古屋不二パークホテル	052-962-2289
Nagoya Grand H. ナゴヤグランドホテル	052-451-0688
Nagoya Hilton 名古屋ヒルトン	052-212-1111

Nagoya-Kanayama Washington H.
名古屋金山ワシントンホテル　052-322-1111

Nagoya Kankō H. 名古屋観光ホテル　052-231-7711

Nagoya Kasadera Washington H.
名古屋笠寺ワシントンホテル　052-612-0001

Nagoya Kokusai H. 名古屋国際ホテル　052-961-3111

Nagoya-marunouchi Tōkyū Inn
名古屋丸ノ内東急イン　052-202-0109

Nagoya Miyako H. 名古屋都ホテル	052-571-3211
Nagoya Plaza H. 名古屋プラザホテル	052-951-6311
Nagoya-sakae Tōkyū Inn 名古屋栄東急イン	052-251-0109
Nagoya Shanpia H. 名古屋シャンピアホテル	052-203-5858
Nagoya Summit H. 名古屋サミットホテル	052-451-0333
Nagoya Terminal H. 名古屋ターミナルホテル	052-561-3751
Nagoya Tōkyū H. 名古屋東急ホテル	052-251-2411
New Plaza H. ニュープラザホテル	052-951-6431
Park Side H. パークサイドホテル	052-971-1131

Sun Heights H. Nagoya
サンハイツホテル名古屋　052-201-6011

Sun H. Nagoya サンホテル名古屋　052-971-2781

〔YOKKAICHI CITY　四日市市〕

Chisan H. Yokkaichi チサンホテル四日市　0593-52-3211

H. Castle Inn Yokkaichi
ホテルキャッスルイン四日市　0593-54-2200

H. Sunroute Yokkaichi
ホテルサンルート四日市　0593-51-32…

Shin Yokkaichi H. 新四日市ホテル	0593-52-61…
Yokkaichi Miyako H. 四日市都ホテル	0593-52-41…

〔SUZUKA CITY　鈴鹿市〕

Central H. セントラルホテル　0593-79-32…

H. Green Palace Suzuka
ホテルグリーンパレス鈴鹿　0593-88-32…

Suzuka Circuit H. 鈴鹿サーキットホテル	0593-78-11…
Suzuka Green H. 鈴鹿グリーンホテル	0593-87-18…
Suzuka Kokusai H. 鈴鹿国際ホテル	0593-78-75…

〔ISE-SHIMA　伊勢志摩〕

H. Shima Spain-mura ホテル志摩スペイン村	05995-7-35…
H. Toba Kowakien ホテル鳥羽小湧園	0599-25-32…
Ise City H. 伊勢シティホテル	0596-28-21…
Ise Kokusai H. 伊勢国際ホテル	0596-23-01…
Ise-Shima Royal H. 伊勢志摩ロイヤルホテル	05995-5-21…
Nemunosato 合歓の郷	05995-2-11…
Shima Kankō H. 志摩観光ホテル	05994-3-12…
Toba Grand H. 鳥羽グランドホテル	0599-25-414…
Toba Kokusai H. 鳥羽国際ホテル	0599-25-312…
Toba Royal H. 鳥羽ロイヤルホテル	0599-25-61…
Toba Seaside H. 鳥羽シーサイドホテル	0599-25-515…

Japanese Inn Group
ジャパニーズ・イン・グループ

〔yōto 京都〕

tsubaya Ryokan 松葉屋旅館	075-351-4268	
nsion Arashiyama
ペンション嵐山嵯峨野	075-881-2294
nsion Higashiyama ペンション東山祇園	075-882-1181
nsion Station Kyōto	
ペンション・ステーション京都	075-882-6200
erside Takase (Annex Kyōka)	
リバーサイド高瀬	075-351-7920
okan Hinomoto 旅館ひのもと	075-351-4563
okan Hiraiwa/Annex Hiraiwa	
旅館平岩/アネックス平岩	075-351-6748
okan Kyōka 旅館京花	075-371-2709
okan Mishima (Mishima Shrine)	
旅館みしま	075-551-0033
okan Murakamiya 旅館村上家	075-371-1260
okan Ohto 京の宿鴨東	075-541-7803
okan Rakuchō 旅館洛頂	075-721-2174
okan Seiki 旅館晴輝	075-551-4911

〔saka 大阪〕

su-so Ryokan えびす荘旅館	06-643-4861

〔Sakai 堺〕

Rinkai Hotel Kitamise 臨海ホテル北店	0722-47-1111

〔Nara 奈良〕

Ryokan Hakuhō 旅館白鳳	0742-26-7891
Ryokan Matsumae 旅館松前	0742-22-3686
Ryokan Seikan-sō 旅館晴観荘	0742-22-2670

〔Ōtsu 大津〕

Ryokan Tsukinoya 月乃家山荘	0775-33-3551

〔Nagoya 名古屋〕

Ōyone Ryokan 大米旅館	052-936-8788
Ryokan Meiryu 旅館名龍	052-331-8686

〔Ise-Shima 伊勢志摩〕

Hoshide Ryokan 星出館	0596-28-2377
Ryokan Ishiyama-sō 旅館石山荘	05995-2-1527

Youth Hostels
ユースホステル

ōto Utano Y.H.	
京都宇多野ユースホステル	075-462-2288
goya Y.H. 名古屋ユースホステル	052-781-9845
akafu Hattori-ryokuchi Y.H.	
大阪府服部緑地ユースホステル	06-862-0600

Airlines
航空会社

Aeroflot Russian Int'l Airlines	
アエロフロート・ロシア国際航空	06-271-8471
Air Canada エア・カナダ	06-252-4227
Air China 中国国際航空	06-946-1702
Air France (AF) エールフランス	06-201-5161
Air Hong Kong エアホンコン	0568-28-2181
Air India (AI) エア・インディア	06-264-1781
Air Lanka エアランカ	06-263-0424
Air New Zealand (TE) ニュージーランド航空	06-212-8990
Alitalia Airlines (AZ) アリタリア航空	06-341-3951
All Nippon Airways (NH) 全日空	
Int'l 国際	06-372-1212
Domestic 国内	06-375-5111
American Airlines (AA) アメリカン航空	06-264-6308
Asiana アシアナ航空	06-229-3939
British Airways (BA) 英国航空	06-347-0771
Canadian Airlines Int'l (CP)	
カナディアン航空	06-346-5591
Cathay Pacific Airways (CX)	
キッセイ・パシフィック航空	06-245-6731
China Airlines 中華航空	
China Eastern Airlines 中国東方航空	06-448-5161
Continental Micronesia Airlines	
コンチネンタルミクロネシア航空	06-251-6015
Egypt Air (MS) エジプト航空	06-341-1575
Finnair (AY) フィンランド航空	06-347-0888
Garuda Indonesian Airways (GA)	
ガルーダ・インドネシア航空	0724-56-5260
Iberia Airlines (IB) イベリア航空	06-347-7201
Japan Airlines (JL) 日本航空	
Int'l 国際	06-203-1212
Domestic 国内	06-201-1231
Japan Air System (JD) 日本エアシステム	06-241-5511
Japan Asia Airways (EG) 日本アジア航空	06-223-2222
KLM Royal Dutch Airlines (KL)	
KLMオランダ航空	0724-56-5200
Korean Air (KE) 大韓航空	06-264-3311
Lufthansa German Airlines (LH)	
ルフトハンザ・ドイツ航空	06-341-4966

Malaysian Airline System (MH)	
マレーシア航空	06-634-772
Pakistan Int'l Airlines (PK)	
パキスタン国際航空	06-341-310
Philippine Airlines (PR) フィリピン航空	06-444-254
Qantas Airways (QF)	
カンタス・オーストラリア航空	06-262-169
	0120-20702
Royal Nepal Airlines	
ロイヤル・ネパール航空	06-229-254
Sabena Belgian World Airlines (SN)	
サベナベルギー航空	06-341-808
Scandinavian Airlines (SK)	
スカンジナビア航空	06-348-022
Singapore Airlines (SQ) シンガポール航空	0724-56-501
Swiss Air Transport (SR) スイス航空	06-345-785
Thai Airways Int'l (TG) タイ国際航空	06-202-516
Turkish Airlines トルコ航空	0724-56-528
United Airlines (UA) ユナイテッド航空	06-271-595
UTA French Airlines (UT) UTAフランス航空	06-345-061
Varig Brazilian Airlines (RG)	
ヴァリグ・ブラジル航空	06-243-387
Vietnam Airlines ベトナム国営航空	06-533-578

Organizations of Int'l Cultural Exchange
国際文化交流団体

mmemorative Asso. for the Japan World Exposition
1970) 日本万国博覧会記念協会 06-877-3331
mamatsu Asso. for Int'l Communications & Exc-
anges 浜松国際交流協会 0534-52-1111
l Cultural Institute (ICI)
際文化交流協会 06-201-5236
l Women's Asso. of Ōsaka
阪国際婦人協会 0726-25-0727
an Asso. and Asian Friendship Society/Japan
ジア協会・アジア友の会 06-341-0587
an-China Friendship Assoc. of Ōsaka Prefecture
阪府日本中国友好協会 06-363-0841
nsai Int'l Students Institute
西国際学友会 06-361-0033
vanis Club of Ōsaka 大阪キワニスクラブ 06-448-3870
be Int'l Association 神戸国際交流協会 078-303-0030
oto Int'l Cultural Association Inc.
京都国際文化協会 075-751-8958
oto Int'l Student House
京都「国際学生の家」 075-771-3648
oto Unesco Association
京都ユネスコ協会 075-241-1823
goya Int'l Center 名古屋国際センター 052-581-5678
aka Chamber of Commerce & Industry
大阪商工会議所 06-944-6400
aka Int'l Festival Society
大阪国際フェスティバル協会 06-227-1061
aka 21st Century Association
大阪21世紀協会 06-942-2001
D Foundation ピー・エイチ・ディー協会 078-351-4892
ga Int'l Friendship Association
滋賀国際友好親善協会 0775-26-0931

Shimazu Science Foundation
島津科学技術振興財団 075-251-2812
Soroptimist Int'l of the Americas, Inc. Japan Region
国際ソロプチミスト・アメリカ・日本リジョン 075-341-8825
Suntory Foundation サントリー文化財団 06-444-1381
Takeda Science Foundation
武田科学振興財団 06-308-7418
The Committee for Int'l Contact
国際交流委員会 075-415-0228
Urasenke Foundation 今日庵(裏千家) 075-431-3111
YMCA Int'l Program Center
YMCA国際・社会奉仕センター 06-344-1717
Young Women's Christian Asso. of Ōsaka
大阪キリスト教女子青年会 06-361-0838

Consulates
領事館

〔ŌSAKA 大阪〕

Australia オーストラリア	06-941-9271
Belgium ベルギー	06-391-9432
Canada カナダ	06-212-4910
China 中華人民共和国	06-445-9481
France フランス	06-946-6181
India インド	06-261-7299
Indonesia インドネシア	06-252-9823
Italy イタリア	06-949-2970
Korea (South) 大韓民国	06-213-1401
Mexico メキシコ	06-538-4630
Netherlands オランダ	06-944-7272
New Zealand ニュージーランド	06-942-9016
Philippines フィリピン	06-910-7881
Russian Fed. ロシア連邦	06-848-3451
Singapore シンガポール	06-261-5131

Switzerland スイス	06-344-7671
Thailand タイ	06-243-5563
United Kingdom イギリス	06-281-1616
U. S. A. アメリカ合衆国	06-315-5900

〔KŌBE 神戸〕

Germany ドイツ	078-857-9961
Korea (South) 大韓民国	078-221-485
Panama パナマ	078-392-3361

〔NAGOYA 名古屋〕

Australia オーストラリア	052-211-0630
Brazil ブラジル	052-222-1077
Canada カナダ	052-972-0450
Korea (South) 大韓民国	052-935-9221
U. S. A. アメリカ合衆国	052-203-4011

Tourist Information Center
ツーリスト・インフォメーション・センター

Kyōto 京都	075-371-5649
Ōsaka 大阪	06-305-3311
Nara 奈良	0742-22-3900
Nagoya 名古屋	052-641-4301

Kyoto Int'l Conference Hall
国立京都国際会館   075-791-3111

関西二ヵ国語アトラス
KYOTO-OSAKA
A Bilingual Atlas

1992年 9 月15日　第 1 刷発行
1996年11月11日　第 2 刷発行

編　者　梅田　厚

発行者　野間佐和子

発行所　講談社インターナショナル株式会社
〒112　東京都文京区音羽 1-17-14
電話：03-3944-6493

印刷所　大日本印刷株式会社

製本所　株式会社 堅省堂

定価はカバーに表示してあります。

Printed in Japan
ISBN 4-7700-1610-7

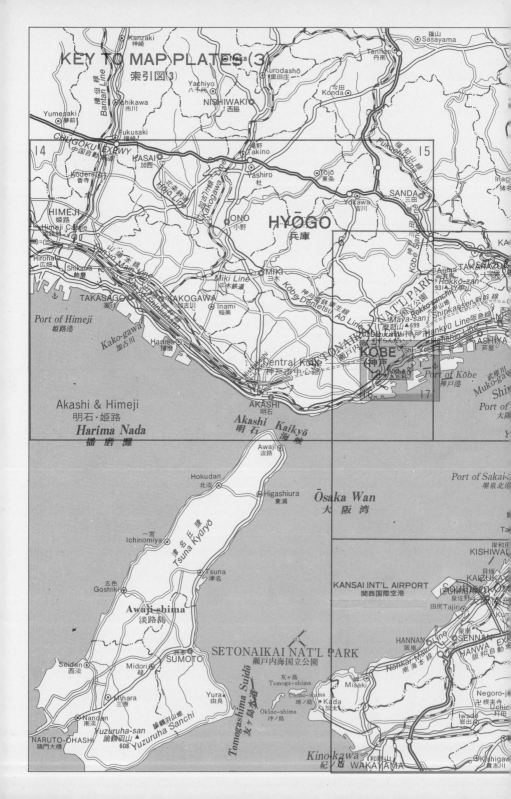

KEY TO MAP PLATES (3)
索引図(3)

14 | 15

HYŌGO
兵庫

Kanzaki
神崎

Sasayama
篠山

Yachiyo
八千代

Kurodashō
黒田庄

Tannan
丹南

NISHIWAKI
西脇

Konda
今田

Fukusaki
福崎

Takino
滝野

Nōjō
東条

Inac

Yashiro
社

Yumesaki
夢前

Ichikawa
市川

Kōdera
香寺

KASAI
加西

SANDA
三田

Yokawa
吉川

KA

CHUGOKU EXPWY
中国自動車道

HIMEJI
姫路

Himeji Castle
姫路城

ONO
小野

TAKARAZUK

Arima
有馬

Rokko-zan
931 六甲山

Hirohata
広畑

MIKI
三木

Miki Line
三木鉄道

Maya-san Shinkansen 新幹線
摩耶山

NAT'L PARK

Shikama
飾磨

TAKASAGO
高砂

KAKOGAWA

Inami
稲美

Rokko-zanchi
六甲山地

Hankyū Line 阪急線

ASHIYA

Port of Himeji
姫路港

Kako-gawa
加古川

Hanima
播磨

Kobe Dentetsu Aō Line
神戸電鉄粟生線

Suzurandai
鈴蘭台

Hanshin Line
阪神線

Shin-Ko

Central Kobe
神戸市中心部

KŌBE
神戸

Shin-Kobe
新神戸

Muko-ga
武庫川

Akashi & Himeji
明石・姫路

AKASHI
明石

Port of Kōbe
神戸港

Shi

Port of

Harima Nada
播磨灘

Akashi Kaikyō
明石海峡

Ō

Awaji
淡路

Port of Sakai
堺泉北港

Hokudan
北淡

Higashiura
東浦

Ōsaka Wan
大阪湾

Ichinomiya
一宮

Tsuna Kyūryō
津名丘陵

KISHIWAD
岸和田

KAIZUKA

Tsuna
津名

KANSAI INT'L AIRPORT
関西国際空港

IZUMISAN

Goshiki
五色

田尻 Tajiri
田尻

Awaji-shima
淡路島

HANNAN
阪南

SENNA

Seidan
西淡

Midori
緑

SUMOTO
洲本

SETONAIKAI NAT'L PARK
瀬戸内海国立公園

Misaki
岬

HANWA EX
阪和自動車

Nankai Main Line
南海本線

Mihara
三原

Yura
由良

Tomoga-shima
地ノ島

Kada
加太

Negoro-ji
根来寺

Nandan
南淡

Chino-shima
地ノ島

Okino-shima
沖ノ島

Iwade
岩出

NARUTO-OHASHI
鳴門大橋

Yuzuruha-san
諭鶴羽山
608

Yuzuruha Sanchi
諭鶴羽山地

Tomogashima Suidō
友ヶ島水道

Kino-kawa
紀ノ川

WAKAYAMA
和歌山

Kishigaw
貴志川

Kishigawa